CONTENTS

Olympic NP

• North Cascades NP

CANADA

• Glacier NP

• Mount Rainier NP

WASHINGTON

MONTANA

OREGON

IDAHO

• Crater Lake NP

• Yellowstone NP

• Grand Teton NP

WYOMING

• Redwood NP

Lassen
Volcanic NP •

NEVADA

UTAH

• Rocky Mountain NP

Great Basin NP •

COLORADO

Yosemite NP
•

Capitol
Reef NP •

Arches NP

• Canyonlands NP

CALIFORNIA

Kings
Canyon NP •

• Sequoia NP

• Bryce Canyon NP

• Zion NP

• Mesa Verde NP

PACIFIC
OCEAN

Grand Canyon NP •

Petrified
Forest NP •

Channel
Islands NP •

ARIZONA

NEW MEXICO

• Carlsbad Caverns NP

4

NP National Park

WHY VISIT IN THE OFF-SEASON ?

Several years ago, I joined three friends on a five-day, 20-mile backpacking adventure into the majestic, primitive, timbered backcountry of Sequoia-Kings Canyon National Park in east-central California. It was late spring on the western slopes of the Sierra Nevada mountain range, and the calendar had not yet summoned summer's full glory, nor summer's warmth. It rained often during those five days. Occasionally, it snowed. One night, while we huddled in our sleeping bags, it began to sleet. We had brought no tents, preferring to rough it (the 40 pounds each of us packed on our back seemed burden enough). The only protection we had from the weather was a large, lightweight plastic tarpaulin stretched between two pine trees over our bunk area. As midnight approached, ice began to form on the plastic, almost collapsing it. Over next morning's breakfast campfire, we wondered aloud who had slept the

least that night, snapping ice off the tarp with numbed fingers.

For five glorious days that spring, we reveled in our wilderness experience. We fished in ice-cold, crystal-clear lakes and streams. We photographed wildlife that seemed totally unafraid of our presence: deer, raccoon, squirrels and, a bit more elusive, one cougar. Walking around a bend in the trail one day, we startled a magnificent golden eagle, perched on a dead tree stump.

Each morning, a squawking Stellar jay was our alarm clock. Each night, whispering pines lulled us to sleep. None of us were seasoned backpackers. But the reward of solitude and witnessing nature's primeval beauty quickly overcame the nervousness of our inexperience. We wore our blisters like badges of honor.

What made that backpacking trip so especially enjoyable was that we scheduled it *off-season*. Schools were still in session; hordes of midsummer tourists had

not arrived; national parks like Sequoia-Kings Canyon had not yet begun to reverberate with the din of thousands of cars, campers, motor homes and motorcycles, blaring radios and the like.

In five days on the trail we met only four or five other humans. Like us, they were backpackers; the only other way to reach our destination was with pack animals. But even the park's more visited areas—Giant Forest, for instance—were most deserted in contrast to the invasion of humanity that lay only a few weeks away. Granted, many of the park's concessions had not yet opened for the season; the lack of crowds simply did not justify them as yet. Yet, like many of the millions of annual visitors to our 49 U.S. national parks, we had come to get *away* from urbanization and its throngs of people. Wilderness, after all, is what the national park idea is all about.

But that was many years ago. Like most of the other 47 United States na-

5

tional parks, Sequoia-Kings Canyon these days is showing signs of people-crush. Our national parks are, as someone aptly put it, being loved to death. Consider that in an average year, more than 265 million people spend at least a part of a day in one of the parks, national monuments or other sites administered by the National Park Service (NPS). And that number is growing year by year—an average of 5 to 7 percent.

That visitation figure represents only the total annual visitation in NPS sites; it does not reflect the peaks and valleys, month-to-month and season-to-season visitor fluctuation. And that can be very significant. As the NPS knows only too well, the visitor load varies markedly throughout the year. The heaviest load occurs when we would most expect it: in midsummer, during the school vacation period. Ironically, summer is the busiest time for most parks and monuments even in hot desert regions, not because people particularly want to be uncomfortable, but because summer, world-wide, is when most people schedule their vacations and travel. And this is exactly why the park visitor who is aware of off-season travel opportunities has many advantages over his more tradition-bound neighbor.

Let's take a look at just one park—Yellowstone in Wyoming—to see how the visitor load varies from season to season. In one recent, fairly typical fiscal year, there were almost 2.4 million total visitors to Yellowstone, counting all months, and all types of visitation; they ranged from the family that spent a few hours marveling at Old Faithful, to visitors who spent several days camping or enjoying other park accommodations. July and August traditionally are Yellow-

stone's busiest months. In those two months alone, the park logged 1,293,255 visitors—or roughly *half* of the number who came during the entire year. By contrast, only 7,295 visitors were counted during the month of November; there were 20,651 in December, only 21,907 in March. In fact, there were less than 90,000 visitors—less than 4 percent of the annual total—who came between mid-December and mid-March, the peak winter "off-season" at this popular national park.

Clearly concerned, the NPS reports that overcrowding is one of the most serious problems facing the entire national park system. It's not so much the total yearly visitor load that creates such a management headache as the fact that the bulk of the load—Yellowstone being only one example—comes during the peak period of summer. Clearly, in terms of visitors, our parks are reaching the saturation point, the wilderness equivalent of urban gridlock.

Why the mushrooming popularity of the parks? Obviously, a growing national population means that there are simply more people looking for the relief and solace of wilderness each year. As any seasoned travel agent knows, costs of travel and unsettling international events—incidents of terrorism, for example—have turned many Americans toward domestic travel at vacation time instead of heading for foreign shores. Too, the past few years have seen a surge of pride—call it patriotism, if you will—in homegrown, American institutions and traditions.

It has been well said that our national parks are to America what Medieval castles and cathedrals are to our European cousins. They are strictly a made-in-

America heritage, a heritage whose inspiration has spread around the globe. Before Yellowstone, there was not a single national park in the entire world. Today, there are more than 1,200 in more than 100 countries. All were inspired by the idea that took root in America a little over a century ago.

It was perhaps natural that in a young nation like the United States, the national park idea could be planted, take root and survive. In the late 19th Century, when some European castles and cathedrals were already very old, the United States—its sprawling West especially—was still a largely wild, unsettled, untamed place. Buffalo still roamed many American prairies. Grizzlies were abundant in Western forests. Millions of acres were still covered with forests, lofty mountains, geologically spectacular canyons that had not yet felt human imprint. Today, the more than 330 NPS units—parks, monuments, seashore and recreation areas, and historic sites—cover 89 million acres in all 50 states plus Guam and the Virgin Islands.

Many remedies have been proposed for the national park overcrowding dilemma: required reservations, prohibition of automobile traffic in the most crowded areas, further restrictions on campgrounds, hiking trails and other facilities are only three prospects on the horizon. Already, supply and demand has imposed its own restraints on park visitation in peak periods, as anyone who has tried to visit California's magnificent Yosemite National Park in July or August, as just one example, can attest.

In 1978, Congress adopted the National Parks and Recreation Act which, among other things, directed NPS park managers to determine "carrying capacities" at all 48 national parks; that is, to determine how many people each park can ultimately accommodate at any one time before reaching the wilderness "gridlock" that many fear is possible. One recurring suggestion is to encourage more people to visit their parks off-season: fall, winter and spring.

To many, the term "off-season" has a negative ring to it, suggesting something less than best, something missing, a less-than-perfect option. For myself and many others, nothing could be further from the truth. In national park terminology, "off-season" is strictly a people term: more people in summer, fewer in fall, winter and spring. It does not refer to the quality of the wilderness experience or what parks have to offer. Off-season in the national parks of the West can be, literally, the best of times.

What are the specific advantages of visiting parks off-season? The most obvious one is, of course, fewer people. Fewer people doesn't mean only more elbow room for human visitors. It means a quieter, less disturbed environment for wildlife as well. Generally, I've seen more animals and birds off-season in national parks than during peak periods, merely because they weren't as upset by so many humans. In the northern mountain parks of the West, winter snow forces many animals instinctively to migrate to lower regions. This makes them more accessible to the visitor's eye and camera.

As a photography enthusiast, I have found that winter especially enhances photographic opportunities in parks of the West, particularly in the canyonlands. Gone is summer's haze; rock formations millions of years old stand out in brilliant color, sometimes powdered

with new-fallen snow, just waiting to be captured on film or on the artist's canvas.

Varying on the calendar from park to park depending upon elevation and latitude, the spring wildflower season is a spectacle to behold throughout the West—another good reason to avoid summer and its crowds. If you want to see waterfalls cascading at their spectacular best, spring is the time to go. In colder climates, winter is too chilly, for me at least, for water sports such as swimming, canoeing, river rafting or waterskiing. Yet there are parks in the West where one can enjoy these activities year around, as this book will show.

On the other hand, snow sports obviously enjoy their greatest popularity in winter and early spring. If skiing, snowshoeing or sledding is your pleasure, you'll avoid the summer months and plan to visit after the first winter storm drapes its white mantle on the landscape.

There are fewer insects as the season grows colder, and fishing improves. And I for one like to plan a fall visit just to watch nature's spectacular show of forest color.

With fewer people to worry about, rangers have more time to answer questions, and the waiting lines at campgrounds, parking lots, stores and restaurants grow dramatically shorter when the crowds leave after Labor Day weekend. In some parks, services and accommodations are cut back in the off-season. That's due to both economics and weather. Smaller crowds simply do not justify keeping many facilities open in the off-season (which is exactly why I and many others like to visit at that time) and, in northern and high elevation parks, winter weather is too severe.

Off-season vacationing, then, is not for everyone, especially for those who insist on all the comforts of home while away from it. Or those who expect perfect weather. There is no nightlife in our national parks, except that provided by nature. There are no Disneylands, gambling casinos or rock bands. So, if you are seeking information on that kind of vacation, this is not your book. It is a guide to the *natural* West, of wilderness, wide open spaces, particularly those places which can best be visited and savored in fall, winter or spring. It's a guide to the West's quiet places where man's imprint is light and signs of civilization are few.

Fortunate is the seeker of nature who lives in or visits the American West. In the Eastern states, less than 10 percent of the land remains in public ownership. But in the large region covered by this book, nearly half of all land is publicly owned. Even eliminating land devoted to military reservations or other nonrecreational use, that's a lot of territory. It is more, in fact, than many nations count within their entire boundaries.

A bit arbitrarily, perhaps, this book concentrates on the states lying west of the 105th meridian. Totaling 1,172,000 square miles in area, they encompass the Southwest states of Arizona and New Mexico, the state of California, the Pacific Northwest represented by Oregon and Washington, and the North-Central states of Idaho, Montana, Wyoming, Colorado, Nevada and Utah.

There are 24 national parks in these states, or nearly half of the 49 found in all the 50 states. There are also 80 other sites administered by the National Park Service, plus millions of acres of national forest, national wildlife refuges and similar lands under the jurisdiction of other fed-

7

SPRINGTIME VISITORS *to Yosemite National Park will have many opportunities to see meadows of bistort such as these and other wildflowers, opportunities they might miss in the height of summer. This scene is in Crane Flat.*

8

Bill Neill

eral departments and agencies. Some states have major state park systems. Possibly nowhere else in the world is there as much outdoor activity and diversity as in the West.

Again, for convenience, *Off-Season* is arranged to take the reader on a leisurely, clockwise circuit of the West. There are five sections, starting in California and winding up in New Mexico and Arizona after a trip that literally extends from Mexico to Canada and from the Pacific Ocean to the Great Plains.

Off-Season is planned for the reader who travels in his own motor vehicle: automobile, recreational vehicle or camper. Tour buses serve some national parks, but parks with airports even close by, anywhere in the NPS system, are rare. The automobile has served our national parks since 1916 when the first road was built through a park in the West. The majority of visitors still vacation this way.

In the West, only Channel Islands National Park, lying off the Southern California coast, cannot be reached by automobile. So while Channel Islands is a delightful and inspiring place to visit any time of year, including off-season, a description of it is reluctantly omitted from this book.

Idaho as yet does not have a national park. However, there are other NPS sites in this state worthy of consideration by the off-season visitor. Important, non-park NPS sites are described briefly in the listing which follows each of the regional sections.

Volcanism, for instance, is the theme of Craters of the Moon National Monument, 18 miles west of Arco, Idaho. Obviously not as heavily visited as Yellowstone, Yosemite or Grand Can-

yon National Parks, the monument's collection of volcanic cones, craters, lava flows and caves nevertheless attracts its share of passersby off-season as well as in midsummer. Craters of the Moon is not on or near any major highway. Yet it *is* only 45 miles as the eagle flies from the popular Idaho winter resort of Sun Valley. For a snow buff whose secondary interest is volcanism, therefore, planning a visit to both places in one trip makes a lot of sense, especially since the Blizzard Mountain Ski Area lies practically at the monument's doorstep.

Maps are included with each of the five regional book sections. These are not intended as detailed road maps, merely as guides to acquaint the reader with the location of Western national parks, important cities, and major highways. For trip planning, travelers should always obtain up-to-date maps of the states to be visited. For further information about specific sites, a list of cooperative park associations is also included.

If you are visiting by car, especially in areas where there is winter snow and where driving conditions may be hazardous, carrying tire chains and other basic emergency equipment is a wise precaution. Especially at winter's peak, many lodges, hotels, restaurants and similar facilities will be closed. Checking ahead is important.

From whatever direction you arrive at a national park, try if possible to make your first stop at the visitor center, operated by the National Park Service. Staffed by helpful park rangers and, in some cases, dedicated volunteers, these centers are gold mines of information for in-park visiting. Larger parks may have more than one visitor center; some also have museums. Maps, brochures, book-

lets, books, exhibits, bird and wildlife lists, historical information—all are available, at most, for a small fee.

Admittedly no regular visitor to national parks, California-born writer John Steinbeck nevertheless experienced awe and admiration when in their presence. "They enclose," he wrote in *Travels With Charley*, "the unique, the spectacular, the astounding—the greatest waterfall, the deepest canyon, the highest cliff, the most stupendous works of man and nature."

In the West, especially, there's no better description of these forested, canyoned, rock-ribbed oases of solitude and silence in one of the world's most highly developed nations, more so off-season than on.

9

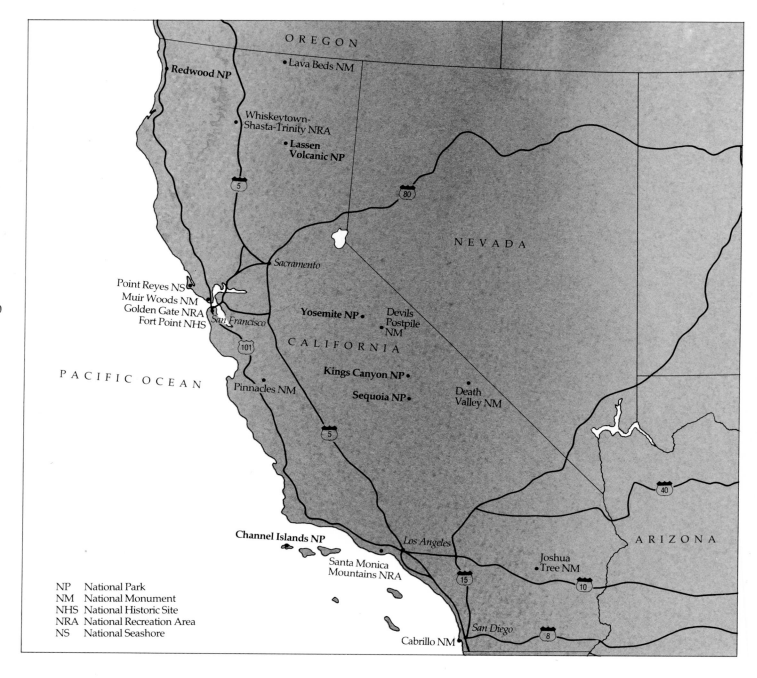

10

OREGON

• Lava Beds NM

Redwood NP

Whiskeytown-
Shasta-Trinity NRA

• **Lassen
Volcanic NP** •

5

80

NEVADA

Sacramento

Point Reyes NS
Muir Woods NM
Golden Gate NRA
Fort Point NHS

San Francisco

101

Yosemite NP •

Devils
Postpile
NM

CALIFORNIA

PACIFIC OCEAN

Pinnacles NM

Kings Canyon NP •

Sequoia NP •

Death
Valley NM

5

40

Channel Islands NP •

Los Angeles

ARIZONA

Santa Monica
Mountains NRA

Joshua
Tree NM •

15

10

San Diego

Cabrillo NM •

8

NP   National Park
NM   National Monument
NHS   National Historic Site
NRA   National Recreation Area
NS   National Seashore

CALIFORNIA

SEQUOIA-KINGS CANYON, YOSEMITE, LASSEN VOLCANIC & REDWOOD NATIONAL PARKS

It has been said that California is as much a state of the mind as a State of the Union. It has also been called a "state of intricate design," a place of "astonishments, contradictions and miracles." Travel writers invariably comment first on California's contrasts and extremes; one dog-eared cliché describes how, in the span of a single afternoon, one may surf in the Pacific Ocean and snow ski on a pine-covered mountain slope, leisurely driving from one to the other without breaking the speed limit. What is perhaps surprising about these statements is that all happen to be true. California is a land of such superlatives—geographic, historic, cultural, political, ethnic—that it demands an entire section of its own.

Considering the geographic potpourri that is California, it seems little wonder that it is not *many* states instead of one.

In California are examples of almost every geologic process known on earth. Climate varies from subtropic to arctic. And, looking around, it's not difficult to understand why it has been named the Golden State. It was gold in the earth—more than $2 billion worth, all told—that triggered one of history's greatest human migrations. Gold is also the color of California's state flower, the poppy, which en masse is a visual feast in the spring. Gold, too, in the leaves of sycamores and aspens, is what draws admiring thousands to California foothills and mountains after summer's end.

No doubt about it, California is big, complex, enigmatic and supremely beautiful. In terms of people, it emerged in midcentury as the nation's most populous state; 25 million Americans now call California their home, and only Alaska and Texas surpass California in area. Give or take an acre lost or gained now and then as the Pacific sculpts and resculpts the curving, 1,100-mile long California shoreline, the state sprawls over 156,297 square miles.

Despite the crush of humanity, this western state remains a treasure trove for lovers of the outdoors. Within its borders are 30,000 miles of rivers (some not yet tamed), 5,000 lakes, a seacoast ranging from low, sandy beaches to ragged cliffs and rocky headlands. Two of North America's mightiest mountain ranges, the Sierra Nevada and the Cascades, reach at least a part of their length through California. In California are examples of both "high" and "low" deserts, of volcanic peaks and plateaus, and of a broad, alluvial valley wider and longer than some states. In California, too, are trees old enough to have witnessed Christ's birth, more plant species than in the entire Northeastern United States, and both the largest state park and the largest national monument.

Californians are outdoor addicts. It is reported that one out of every three families owns some type of recreational vehicle and in peak season, outdoor California is overcrowded. Through the years, "reservations only" have more and more become a fact of California life.

Yet the Golden State is so large, so varied, and its landscape so tolerant that uncrowded places are still not impossible to find. Looking for them in fall, winter or spring only increases the odds.

California can be divided into five major "parts," or landforms, and the state includes at least one example of terrain found anywhere in the world. In elevation, the state climbs from 282 feet below sea level in Death Valley, the lowest point in the United States, to 14,495-foot-high Mount Whitney, highest peak in the conterminous states. These extremes lie less than 60 miles apart.

Perhaps California's single most impressive physical feature is the Sierra Nevada mountain range, which occupies one fifth of the state's total land area. Varying from 40 to 80 miles in width, the Sierra extends nearly 430 miles from northwest to southeast. The largest single block of granite in the United States, it is a mountain range nearly as extensive as the Alpine system of Europe. Naturalist John Muir, whose name is synonymous with the Sierra, called these mountains the "Range of Light."

The Sierra covers 27,000 square miles. It encompasses 6,200-foot-high Lake Tahoe, an aquamarine jewel surrounded by 9,000- and 10,000-foot mountain peaks, three of California's five national parks (Yosemite, Sequoia and Kings Canyon) as well as all or parts of six national forests.

The High Sierra is a magnificent example of glaciation. Consisting largely of clean-swept, polished rock, it is backcountry unexcelled in the United States: more than 1,200 lakes and numerous canyons, all mantled by a sky of incredible blueness and extreme clarity.

The Cascade Range is California's sec-ond major mountain range. It extends southward from British Columbia to the northern end of the Sierra. Volcanic in origin, the Cascades include Mount Shasta, 14,161 feet high, and Mount Lassen, 10,457 feet. Until Mount St. Helens in the state of Washington stole the headlines in 1980, Lassen held the distinction of being the only volcano in the contiguous 48 states to erupt in modern times. Lassen, a national park since 1916, literally blew its top in 1914.

California counts two other mountain systems within its borders. With elevations ranging from 2,000 to 4,000 feet, the Coast Range (actually a *system* of ranges) extends 400 miles northwest-southeast from Oregon's Klamath Mountains into Southern California. A few peaks exceed 6,000 feet. Closest to the Pacific Ocean of California's mountains, they are an old landmass of modified sedimentary and igneous rock that has been repeatedly folded, uplifted, faulted and eroded. One of the most spectacular sections of the Coast Range runs 80 miles to form the eastern backdrop of California's Big Sur. The Tehachapi Mountains extend east-west across the southern end of the Great Central Valley, separating the valley from Southern California.

The valley itself, the second major landform, is a sprawling, banana-shaped alluvial plain lying between the Sierra and the Coast Range mountains. It covers about 25,000 square miles and extends from Redding on the north to near Bakersfield on the south. Before the arrival of the white man, great forests of oak grew along the banks of valley streams, and tule marshes were thick in river deltas. There were dozens of wild animals and many plant species. Though most of the valley has yielded to crops of rice, cotton, oranges, tomatoes and lettuce, the foothills and mountains that flank it still support one of the most varied plant and animal populations in the United States.

In addition to the seacoast (see related article) California has three other important landforms. Two are deserts. The Mojave, northeast of Los Angeles, and the Colorado, at the southeast corner of the state, are both parts of the sprawling Basin and Range Region of the West, which extends from the Mexican border north to Oregon and southern Idaho, and east as far as central Utah.

Death Valley, the country's largest national monument (2,067,628 acres), is one of the best-known features of the Mojave Desert, which in total covers more than one sixth of California. The Colorado Desert—lower, hotter in summer and colder in winter than the Mojave—is termed by some scientists as a part of the Sonoran Desert, which covers a large section of northern Mexico.

The fifth and final landform, the volcanic Modoc Plateau, might be called "The Forgotten California." Covering a large portion of northeast California, it is a brooding, somber, lonesome land, perhaps the least visited area in a state in which tourism is an important economic asset. With a total population of only about 25,000, the plateau is in fact larger than any of the nation's nine smallest states. It is a forbidding place where widespread basaltic lava flows a million or more years ago left a stony soil unsuited for anything but the subsistence grazing to which the plateau owes its main economy today.

The plateau averages about 4,500 feet in elevation, rising as high as 10,000 feet. And despite the fact that the area generally is passed up by most tourists, Lava Beds National Monument, near Tulelake, makes a worthwhile destination for those interested in volcanism.

Prehistoric Indians were the first humans to settle in California thousands of years before the white man. It is likely they arrived via a land bridge which once connected present-day Alaska with Siberia on the Asian-European continent. They settled first in today's Pacific Northwest, gradually migrating south to warmer environments.

Neither nomadic nor warlike, some were hunters, most were food gatherers, subsisting on roots, berries, herbs, nuts, and seafood that was easily available. Acorns were a favorite staple with some groups. Coastal tribes used nets and traps to catch fish or small game, and all of California's earliest inhabitants enjoyed a close communal relationship with nature.

California's human drama after the Indians is something John Steinbeck managed to sum up in four sentences in *East of Eden:* "Then the hard, dry Spaniards came exploring through. They collected souls as they collected jewels. Then the Americans came—more greedy because there were more of them. They took the land, remade the laws to make their titles good."

If Steinbeck's summation is unsparingly terse, it is at least chronologically accurate. California's post-Indian history can be divided into three distinct periods: the 16th Century Spanish discoverers, the 17th and 18th Century Mexican colonizers and settlers after Mexico's revolt from Spain, and the modern American period. There are many overlaps in the chronology, and there are occasional interlopers; even the Russians, for instance, were Californians for a brief period, as well-preserved architectural remains of their Fort Ross fur-trading colony, on the northern California shoreline, will prove.

The dawn of "modern" California is precise. It was on January 24, 1848, when a lumberman-sawyer named James Marshall spotted a few flakes of a dullish yellow substance in a millrace near Coloma on the North Fork of the American River. The Great California Gold Rush, and California's rapid rise to world prominence, was on.

With so much to do and see in this historic, scenic state where wilderness does indeed still exist in unspoiled abundance, weather and climate are naturally of concern to travelers. Ironically, there is no such thing as "California weather," and only by first deciding on a specific destination can preparation be made for the capriciousness of nature.

In latitude, California lies about midway between the Equator and the North Pole. Its climate seems to draw inspiration from both.

In recent geologic times, even as recently as the 15th and 16th Centuries, the climate was somewhat warmer and more humid than it is today. But it hasn't changed *much*, and it is climate, perhaps more than anything else, that lures both visitors and permanent immigrants each year in record numbers.

Because of the state's topographical extremes and greatly varying local features, weather conditions may vary widely at points only a few miles apart. Wise is the traveler, then, who plans tomorrow's outing not by the national six o'clock TV forecast, but by monitoring what the local weather wizards see in their meteorological crystal ball.

Three generalizations can be made, however, about annual weather patterns in California, particularly those involving precipitation.

The amount of precipitation *decreases* from north to south; it *increases* with elevation, and it is greater on the west sides of mountain ranges than on the east.

Summing it up, traveling off-season in California does not present the kinds of weather hazards encountered in, say, the blizzard-prone Great Plains states or even in higher altitudes of the Rocky Mountains in winter. For the national park visitor, high mountain passes may present a problem. Spectacular though they may be under snowdrifts, many of California's east-west mountain passes close down in winter. The extreme heat of desert areas may deter summer travelers from places like Death Valley, on the other hand, but visiting in late fall, winter or spring is delightful.

Aside from weather considerations and the long driving distances in the nation's second longest state, visiting outdoor California is a relatively easy affair. California has one of the country's best state road systems, and it is cross-laced with freeways of the interstate system as well. Interstate 5, for instance, now whisks the motorist all the way from the Mexican border to Canada without the annoyance of a traffic signal. But freeways are *not* the way to visit national parks, in California or elsewhere, and if you take I-5 the length of California, what you'll see mostly is a long, uninteresting expanse of the Great Central Valley. If you are in a hurry, I-5 is fine, but to see any of the state's national parks, the spectacular seacoast, the historic Mother Lode, the cool wintertime beauty of the southern deserts or John Muir's incom-

13

parable Range of Light, some detouring and doglegging will be necessary.

Sequoia-Kings Canyon and Yosemite National Parks are near neighbors. You can reach either only a few miles drive east of I-5 in the San Joaquin Valley. From Yosemite (northern of the two parks) to Lassen Volcanic National Park, you can save time by returning to I-5, driving north, and then turning east again on highways to Lassen from either Red Bluff or Redding. A more rewarding route, however, is State Hwy. 49, which wends its way leisurely through the Sierra's western foothills from a juncture with State Hwy. 41 near Oakhurst on the south to State Hwy. 41 northwest of Reno, Nevada. A substantial portion of Hwy. 49 meanders through the historic gold towns of the Mother Lode country.

An alternative plan is, after visiting Yosemite, to drive westward on one of the many trans-state routes which link the Sierra with the San Francisco Bay area. This would give you an opportunity to visit the Golden Gate National Recreation Area (GGNRA), one of the National Park Service's newest national "urban parks," as well as the Point Reyes National Seashore and other historic and scenic points along coast-hugging State Hwy. 1, which leads to Redwood National Park and its neighboring state redwood parks in California's northwest corner. Here, the lofty *Sequoia sempervirens*, the coast redwood, has been saved and preserved by man's wise intervention. Though a part of the GGNRA is urban, Muir Woods National Monument and the Muir Headlands are not; they are superb examples of how, throughout California, there are still wild, scenic oases of nature practically at the doorstep of crowded cities.

Sequoia-Kings Canyon National Park

Administered as a single unit of the National Park Service, adjoining Sequoia and Kings Canyon National Parks offer a splendid variety of the Sierra's scenic best: lush forests, alpine high country, more than 700 miles of hiking trails, cascading waterfalls, two mighty river canyons, the world's largest trees, jewel-like lakes and flower-bedecked meadows.

Designated as the nation's second national park (after Yellowstone), Sequoia joined the National Park System in 1890. At issue was the survival of its giant *Sequoiadendron giganteum*, hardy survivor of the Ice Age, the world's largest tree and one of its oldest, threatened by the logger's axe. It took another 50 years for Kings Canyon, a showcase of glacial sculpting and the power of water, to become protected.

As neighbors, the two parks now encompass nearly 900,000 acres, attract more than two million visitors each year, and range in elevation from 2,000 feet from their scrub-covered foothills, an explosion of wildflowers in spring, to the 14,495-foot summit of Mount Whitney, highest peak in the contiguous U.S.

Typical of the 430-mile-long Sierra, climate and weather in the parks vary dramatically not only from season to season but from elevation to elevation. Winters are long, ranging from moderate in the foothills to arctic at the summits, many of which reach almost three miles into the sky. On the average, the temperature drops about one degree (Fahrenheit) for each 300 feet of elevation, and precipitation—rain and snow—increase as one travels from lowland to high ground. Sierra snows are

historically heavy; snowpacks average 5 to 10 feet, but in 1969, a record-maker of nearly 36 feet was recorded.

On either end of the crowded summer months and the deep of winter are the times many visitors enjoy best: fall and spring. In fall, hillsides are ablaze in pre-winter forest splendor; cooler temperatures make hiking more comfortable in the foothills which can be sizzling in midsummer. Spring is the time, as John Muir poetically described it, "when the snow melts into music." Although one must prepare for sunshine, rain, fog and snow sometimes on the same day, the spring visitor here finds rivers at their tumbling best, wildlife stirring from winter's slumber and wildflowers in profusion, their variety changing as one ascends from foothill to forest to mountain summit.

It is in the parks' mid-altitude range—the forests—that most visitors gather, and where most facilities and services such as campgrounds, winter sports, food, lodging and interpretive services are found.

Grant Grove is the first reached by motorists arriving from Fresno, on State Hwy. 180. A detached section of Kings Canyon National Park, it marks the beginning of Generals Highway which meanders 46 miles into Sequoia National Park, through Giant Forest and on to Ash Mountain.

The nation's Christmas tree, the General Grant, is a short distance from the Grant Grove Visitor's Center. So is the Centennial Stump, all that is left of a giant sequoia felled for the 1875 World's Fair, and remains of other trees cut down in the park's logging days.

Of all the Sierra's wonders, none intrigues and inspires more than the mighty sequoia. The largest single living

14

Pat O'Hara

IN TERMS *of total wood volume, giant sequoias like this one are the largest living things on earth. The diameters of some of these trees at their base exceed the width of many city streets. The heavy, spongy bark on this specimen is a protection against fire.*

thing on earth, the General Sherman Tree—over 50,000 cubic feet of wood, 275 feet tall, 36 feet at its diameter—is in Giant Forest of Sequoia National Park. It is a living relic whose age is estimated to be between 2,200 and 2,500 years. Giant Forest offers a sampling of the park's many features for the visitor in a hurry. Here, for instance, are not only big trees, but meadows, groves and scenic outlooks that can be reached in a short distance by trail. Especially rewarding is the view from 6,725-foot-high Moro Rock, only a 300-foot climb from a parking lot at the south end of the Giant Forest visitor complex. From this lookout, one may gain a 360-degree panorama including the San Joaquin Valley 6,000 feet below and, to the east, the peaks of the Great Western Divide. Wolverton, in the northeast section of the area, is the center for winter snow sports; the season runs from about November through March.

15

Cedar Grove, in the middle of Kings Canyon National Park, nestles in a heavily forested area on the South Fork of the Kings River. Rocky cliffs vault more than a mile almost straight up at each side. Cedar Grove is also the embarkation point for much of Sequoia-Kings Canyon backcountry hiking. Roaring River Falls, Mist Falls and Zumwalt Meadows are three popular short-range destinations. For the more ambitious, the primitive, lofty Sierra Crest lies to the east beyond. Ranging in elevation from 11,000 to 14,495 feet, there are more than 1,000 glacial lakes in the high country, with classic examples of hanging valleys, glacially polished rock, moraines and related glacial features.

The high country is a stark landscape. Trees are gnarled and stunted, or there are no trees at all. Only the hardiest,

A FULL MOON *sets over the peak of Mount Whitney in Sequoia-Kings Canyon National Park, the tallest peak in the contiguous United States. The mountain is 14,495 feet tall; Mount Denali in Alaska (formerly Mount McKinley) is the highest in the United States.*

Pat O'Hara

most adaptable of animals are seen, and bare granite peaks claw their way up above a landscape more suited to Alaska than California. Here and there are tiny remnants of the huge glaciers that sculpted this land so long ago. Snow and ice linger all year long.

Sequoia-Kings Canyon National Park
Three Rivers, CA 93271, (209) 565-3341
Access: To Sequoia from Visalia, 35 miles east on State Hwy. 198. To Kings Canyon from Fresno, 55 miles east on State Hwy. 180. Generals Highway connects Hwy. 198 and 180; this 2-hour drive passes through Sequoia to Kings Canyon.
Season: Sequoia is open all year; some roads closed during the winter. Kings Canyon's Grant Grove, a detached section of the park, is open year around. Cedar Grove is open only from May through October. The Generals Highway between Grant Grove and Giant Forest may be closed by snow occasionally.
Visitor Centers: Sequoia visitor centers at Ash Mountain and Lodgepole, open all year. Kings Canyon, Grant Grove, open all year. The Cedar Grove center is open from late May to October.
Lodging: Sequoia and Kings Canyon have cabins available through Sequoia-Kings Canyon Hospitality Service, (209) 561-3314. Kings Canyon accommodations at Wilsonia Lodge, (209) 335-2310.
Camping: Sequoia has three campgrounds with trailer space (no hookups). Four campgrounds have limited facilities, no trailers. Three are open all year, others available from April or May through September or October. All are first come, first served except Lodgepole, which requires reservations from Mem-

orial Day to Labor Day (Ticketron Reservations, P.O. Box 2715, San Francisco CA 94126). Kings Canyon has seven campgrounds with normal facilities; most are open May 20–Sept. 15. Sheep Creek in Cedar Grove is open May 1–Nov. 1. All are first come, first served. One is open all year at Grant Grove.

Services: Gas available for Sequoia at Lodgepole, Stony Creek and Three Rivers; in Kings Canyon, at Grant Grove and Cedar Grove. Meals, food and supplies available in Sequoia at Giant Forest, Stony Creek and Lodgepole, and at nearby Three Rivers. In Kings Canyon, meals, food and supplies at Grant Grove, Cedar Grove and Wilsonia.

Activities: Sequoia has hiking, horseback riding, fishing, mountain climbing and both cross-country and downhill skiing. Kings Canyon affords hiking, horseback riding, fishing, mountain climbing and cross-country skiing. Guided nature walks and campfire programs at both parks.

Contact park headquarters for further information on permits, fees, reservations and park regulations.

J F M A M J J A S O N D
Sequoia-Kings Canyon annual visitors, 2,090,000

Yosemite National Park

Historians will correctly recall that Yellowstone, chartered in 1872 and now well into its second century, was the United States' first national park. But without dampening Yellowstone's well-deserved distinction, those who love wilderness and those who struggle to protect it will just as correctly state that the *idea* for national parks may well have started someplace else. The concept of the park philosophy, which since has spread to more than 100 countries, really began almost a decade earlier in the heart of California's incomparable Sierra Nevada mountain range.

It was in 1864 that Congress, heeding warnings that humans had begun to encroach upon the Sierra's magnificent natural treasures, acted to save two small parts of what eventually became one of the largest and most popular of all national parks—Yosemite. President Abraham Lincoln signed the legislation which deeded Yosemite Valley and the Mariposa Groves of giant sequoias to the state of California on the condition ". . . that the premises shall be held for public use, resort, and recreation [and] shall be inalienable for all time."

More than a century has passed since the federal act whose landmark philosophy now has spread around the world. Yet it was evident from the beginning that saving the two areas was not enough; protecting them alone would be a hollow gesture unless a vast watershed around them, upon which the valley and the groves depended for their survival, was not also protected. In 1890, 18 years after Yellowstone officially had become the first national park, the drainage basins of the Tuolumne and Merced Rivers were granted federal protection, while the state continued to administer Yosemite Valley and Mariposa Grove. The year of 1890 is regarded as the official date of the founding of Yosemite National Park, though it wasn't until 1906, when California returned the original gift land, that 1,189-square-mile Yosemite National Park, with some boundary changes, became the park we know today.

It is far more than mere size, however, that accounts for the enormous appeal of this sprawling mountain park which lies about midway down the 430-mile northwest-southeast length of the mighty Sierra. Yosemite is a place with literally something for everyone and a landscape that is unmatched anywhere in the West. With an elevation ranging from 2,000 feet to more than 10,560 feet, it encompasses prime examples of the best of Sierra wildlands: giant sequoia groves, glacier-carved peaks and canyons, domes, two major rivers, serene meadows, hillsides of pine, fir and aspen, huge monoliths of ancient stone. For the outdoorsman, Yosemite offers more than 750 miles of trail; for the motorist, 200 miles of road. Here is a park for the skier, the camper, the history buff and the amateur geologist. Here, too, are secluded places where the most strenuous activity is meditation.

For convenience's sake, the park can be said to offer three major features: Yosemite Valley, the mountain wilderness of the high backcountry, and preserved groves of earth's largest living things, the giant sequoias.

To many visitors, Yosemite Valley *is* Yosemite, characterized by sheer walls, a flat floor through which tumbles the Merced River, by awesome monoliths (one of them—El Capitan—is the world's largest single exposed piece of

17

granite), by waterfalls and quiet, flower-filled meadows. Extending generally east-west across the midsection of the park, Yosemite Valley covers less than one percent of Yosemite's total area. Yet here in a microcosm is what Yosemite—and the Sierra itself—is all about. It's a wonderland that has inspired poet, artist, photographer and naturalist since its discovery more than a century ago.

Yosemite Valley is one of the world's best examples of a valley carved by both glaciers and roaring water, and there is evidence of the work of these giant, ponderous Ice Age land shapers everywhere you look. The U-shape of the valley is itself a glacial trademark. The valley's waterfalls, domes and monoliths are the work of scouring ice, as well as later weathering which exposed the bare, uplifted granite beneath.

The western end of the Merced River Canyon along State Hwy. 140 outside the national park, lay beyond the path of the descending glaciers. The canyon here is V-shaped rather than U-shaped, indicating that it was the Merced River, not glacial ice, that did the cutting and gouging.

Around the valley's rim are Yosemite's famous waterfalls; collectively, they are some of the world's most spectacular. Yosemite Falls plunges 2,425 feet in three stages. A classic example of the "hanging" type of waterfall, it is believed to be the fifth highest waterfall in the world. However, some of the others have little or no water from mid-August to early fall. Spring, when the Sierra snowpack begins to melt, is the best time to view Yosemite's tumbling water show, and if you time your visit before schools close or just after the summer rush, you'll enjoy it even more.

In Yosemite's meadows, wildflowers and flowering shrubs are seen at their best in spring, amidst forests of Douglas fir, ponderosa pine, and incense cedar. You'll see a lot of wildlife, too, especially off-season when crowds are smaller; meadow-browsing mule deer and several species of rodents are the park's most conspicuous mammals. The keen-eyed may also spot bobcat, bear, coyote, raccoon, fox and porcupine. Botanists have counted more than 1,400 species of flowering plants throughout Yosemite, and 37 kinds of native trees.

One of Yosemite National Park's three visitor centers is located in Yosemite Valley, as are the rustic, historic Ahwahnee Hotel, other lodges and visitor services. The Indian Cultural Museum and the Indian Village near the Valley Visitor Center are treasure troves for those intrigued by Sierra Indian history. The Ahwahnee-chee Indians made the valley their home perhaps 4,000 years before its discovery by the white man, subsisting on mammals, birds, fish and acorns (a staple of their diet).

Most roads in Yosemite Valley are one-way, but, due to heavy visitation, those at the eastern end section are closed to automobiles. A free shuttle bus carries visitors on a loop trip around the eastern half of the valley, stopping at convenient spots to trailheads and facilities. A less "peopled" way to see the valley is via one of the foot trails which are part of a 750-mile trail system throughout the national park.

One of the finest views of Yosemite Valley, as well as a place to gain a sweeping, bird's-eye view of the Yosemite high country with its 13,000-foot peaks, is Glacier Point. The 3,200-foot sheer drop from this 7,214-foot-high overlook gives one a view of the entire valley and its famous landmarks. Half Dome is off to the right; Vernal Fall seems within reach; Nevada Fall's thundering water fills the air and, far to the right, are the snow-clad peaks of the Sierra crest. Towering Glacier Point is a 30-mile drive from Yosemite Village, but Glacier Point Road which leads to it is open only in summer. In winter, the road is open only from the park's south entrance to the Badger Pass Ski Area; from that point on, it is snowed-in and accessible only to cross-country skiers and snowshoers.

However, there are three good trails leading out of the valley to Glacier Point. For instance, Four Mile Trail is a three to four hour walk from the valley, climbing 3,200 feet; it's a strenuous hike, with many switchbacks, but the view from the top is well worth it. In winter, Glacier Point is a favorite destination for cross-country skiers, starting at the Badger Pass Ski Area.

Just north of the park's south entrance on Hwy. 41 is Wawona. Built as a trail-side camp by Galen Clark, the first Guardian of the Yosemite Grant, the area retains much of the flavor which recalls Yosemite's past. The Pioneer Yosemite History Center is located here. Stagecoach rides are a part of the living history program, scheduled throughout the summer. The landmark Wawona Hotel is also here. Built in 1879 to accommodate visitors who had come from the San Joaquin Valley to experience the wonders of Sierra wilderness, it is still serving guests.

Located 6.6 miles southeast of Wawona and 35 miles from Yosemite Valley is the Mariposa Grove. Here the largest of the park's three groves of *Sequoiadendron giganteum*—the big trees—is found.

18

(The other two are the Tuolumne and Merced Groves, near Crane Flat.)

The Grizzly Giant in Mariposa Grove is estimated to be 2,700 years old, making it probably the oldest of all known Sequoias. Private vehicles are not allowed beyond the Mariposa Grove parking lot, a rule which became necessary as much to protect the trees as to relieve traffic congestion, especially in midsummer. A free tram system, operating from mid-May to mid-October, allows visitors a close-up look at these ageless wonders.

For many visitors to Yosemite, it is the backcountry wilderness whose siren call is the most compelling. In summer, you can see a lot of the high country by driving across the park on Tioga Road (Hwy. 120). Built as a mining road in 1882–83, even before Yosemite became a national park, it was modernized and realigned in 1961. The road has many scenic turnouts which afford splendid views of meadows, lakes, domes and mountain peaks that 10,000 years ago lay under a blanket of glacial ice. At its highest point—9,945-foot Tioga Pass—you may see the striking contrast of Yosemite forest and canyons to the west, and the desertlike Owens Valley to the east. This is the highest mountain pass open to vehicles in California. The road is closed, however, from the first snow until late spring, and visitors at other times must explore the way John Muir and other Sierra pioneers did—on foot.

One of the most scenic starting places for a Yosemite backcountry expedition is Tuolumne Meadows, at 8,600 feet in elevation the largest subalpine meadow in the entire Sierra. Long a favorite with summer visitors, Tuolumne Meadows is growing in popularity with winter mountaineers. Cross-country skiing is

19

Bill Neill

YOSEMITE FALLS, *framed here by a cluster of cottonwoods, is perhaps the best-known waterfall in Yosemite National Park. It plunges 2,425 feet in three stages. Spring, when the Sierra snowpack begins to melt, is the best time to view these falls.*

A SAMPLING *of Yosemite's beauty, clockwise from above. The snow-capped Kuna Crest is reflected in the small mountain lake of Tioga Tarns; winter drapes a frosting of white on Half Dome (at left) and Cathedral Spires; a view of El Capitan and Half Dome under a cloudy sky in the background; smoke curls from the chimney of the Grove Museum in Upper Mariposa Grove, where snow is banked against the trunk base of a giant*

20

Bill Neill

Pat O'Hara

Pat O'Hara

Bill Neill

sequoia; a gem among national park lodges is
Yosemite's Ahwahnee Hotel, opened in July 1927,
and still serving guests today. The Ahwahnee cost
$1 million to build, and it was an extravagant
undertaking. Interior decor and furnishings alone
cost $250,000, a princely sum in the Twenties,
and more than the cost of some lodges in other
national parks. Its 150-foot-long dining hall can
seat 300 people at one time. El Capitan, believed to
be one of the world's largest single exposed pieces of
granite, forms a dramatic backdrop for the famous
hostelry, dwarfing it in this magnificent setting.

21

Fred Hirschmann

popular throughout the park; there are more than 90 miles of ski-touring trails. Services of the park's ski schools are tailored to both seasoned skiers and novices; the ski season runs from about Thanksgiving until mid-April.

Backpackers heading even higher into the Yosemite backcountry will pass through some of the most spectacular country in the entire West.

Yosemite experiences its peak visiting season in July and August. Off-season, however, the visitor head count decreases dramatically; yet for many, off-season is Yosemite at its best. In spring, western redbud and dogwood, among others, stage a spectacular botanical show, and waterfalls are at their fullest. Winter snow may bury some of summer's familiar landmarks, but the silent crispness of January or February in the Sierra is spellbinding. And in fall, after summer's crowds have gone, hillsides and meadows dazzle the eye in their crimson reds, golden yellows, glorious oranges and lush greens. Whoever complained that California has no seasons doubtless has never been to Yosemite.

Yosemite has a boreal climate—that is, one that relates typically to mountain areas throughout the Northern Hemisphere. Summer days are warm; temperatures at lower elevations may reach 100 degrees F, cooling off at night. Summer skies can be blue and cloudless, especially in the high country, but don't be surprised to be drenched by a thundershower in the warm months.

In winter, temperatures may plummet to as low as 5 or 10 degrees, but usually range between 20 and 40 degrees in Yosemite Valley. Though Yosemite Valley may be entirely snowless in some years, higher elevations receive plenty of snow.

In Spanish, in fact, *Sierra Nevada* means "snowy mountain range." Snowpacks of up to 10 feet have accumulated from high-country storms after only a week, and winter avalanches can occur.

The best bet for seasonal weather information is a current copy of the *Yosemite Guide*, a free park newspaper which also contains current information on interpretive programs, facilities and services, seminars and general park information. It is available at all visitor centers, entrance stations and at most concessioner-operated lodges, stores and other service facilities. Telephone numbers to obtain further information are listed in the *Yosemite Guide*.

Yosemite National Park P.O. Box 577, Yosemite National Park, CA 95389, (209) 372-0200

Access: From Merced, 81 miles east on State Hwy. 140. From Fresno, 94 miles north on State Hwy. 41. From Manteca, east on State Hwy. 120. Hwy. 120 is closed from Lee Vining in winter.

Season: Park open all year. Mariposa Grove Road, Tuolumne Grove Road, Glacier Point Road and Tioga Road closed from mid-November to late May.

Visitor Centers: Yosemite Valley, Tuolumne Meadows, Big Oak Flat entrance. Museum located in Yosemite Indian Cultural Museum and Happy Isles Nature Center in Yosemite Valley; Pioneer Yosemite History Cultural and Hills Studio at Wawona; and Mariposa Grove Museum.

Lodging: In park: Yosemite Valley (year-round); White Wolf, Wawona, Tuolumne Meadows, and five High Sierra camps in summer. Reservations advised at all times for hotels, lodges and cabins. Contact Yosemite Park and Curry Co.,

5410 E. Home, Fresno, CA 93727, or telephone (209) 252-4848. Nearby: Lee Vining, Groveland, El Portal, Wawona, Oakhurst, Fish Camp and Mariposa.

Camping: Many campgrounds throughout the park. Several are open year-around on a first-come, first-served basis. The five Yosemite Valley and Hodgodon Meadows campgrounds require reservations May–September. Reservations may be made eight weeks in advance through Ticketron outlets or by writing to: Ticketron, Dept. R., 401 Hackensack Ave., Hackensack, NJ 07601.

Services: Gas year-round in Yosemite Valley and at Wawona; Tuolumne Meadows and Crane Flat, summer only. Meals, food, gifts and supplies in park: Yosemite Valley, Wawona and El Portal, year-round; White Wolf, Crane Flat, Glacier Point, Tuolumne Meadows and five High Sierra camps in summer. Nearby: Lee Vining, Groveland, El Portal, Wawona, Oakhurst, Fish Camp and Mariposa.

Activities: Driving, hiking, climbing, horseback riding, bird and wildlife watching, swimming, boating (no motors), fishing, alpine and cross-country skiing and backpacking by permit. Photography, bicycling, rafting.

For further information on permits, fees, reservations and park regulations, write or call park headquarters.

J F M A M J J A S O N D
Yosemite annual visitors, 2,285,000

Lassen Volcanic National Park

The date was May 30, 1914. Late that afternoon, a Californian named Bert McKenzie noted something odd: a column of steam and ash had begun to rise suddenly above a mountain peak that had been quiet and serene all the years of his memory. The peak was Lassen, nearly two miles tall, named for an enterprising 19th Century Danish blacksmith, Peter Lassen, who had used it as a landmark to guide immigrant parties into California. Long dormant, volcanic Lassen Peak had at last come to life. It would smolder, sputter, spew and explode with intermittent intensity over the next seven years. Lassen's most violent outburst occurred on May 22, 1915, when lava fragments as big as small automobiles flattened a 3-square-mile area of forest on the east side of the peak and sent a column of warm volcanic mud flowing down the Hat Creek and Lost Creek valleys. A huge cloud, towering 7 miles high, could be seen as far as Sacramento, 170 miles distant; volcanic ash littered the streets of Reno, Nevada, nearly as far.

Unlike that of Mount St. Helens in Washington State in 1980, the Lassen eruption killed no one, and only one injury occurred from the volcano which earlier Indians had appropriately called Fire Mountain or Mountain-ripped-apart. Lassen's awakening did, however, focus worldwide attention on an almost forgotten corner of California where lumbering in the region's magnificent conifer forests had reached an alarming level. Two parts of the Lassen area, Lassen Peak and nearby Cinder Cone, had been designated as national monuments in 1907, seven years before

23

Pat O'Hara

WISPY CLOUDS *form a necklace around the peak of Mount Lassen, reflected in Manzanita Lake. The volcano was named for Peter Lassen, a Danish blacksmith who used the peak as a landmark for California-bound immigrants.*

the eruption. But upgrading to national park status was clearly called for. Listening to the new clamor brought about by the reborn volcano, Congress established Lassen Volcanic National Park, now encompassing 106,000 acres, in 1916.

Lassen Volcanic National Park rises in elevation from 5,300 feet to the summit of Lassen itself at 10,457 feet, at the southern end of the Cascade mountain range near its juncture with the Sierra Nevada range. Extending north into British Columbia, Canada, the Cascades are relatively young mountains born in fire; at least eight of the peaks are volcanic, either extinct, dormant or, like Lassen and Mount St. Helens, active in recent years. A ninth, now Crater Lake National Park in Oregon, last erupted 6,600 years ago; when its walls collapsed, its role in volcanism passed forever into geologic history.

Except that it has no geysers, Lassen Volcanic National Park claims more varied pieces of evidence of volcanism than in any area of comparable size in the world, the more popular, better-known Yellowstone National Park notwithstanding. Best yet, the volcanic debris—cinder cones, lava flows and thermal hot springs such as gurgling, boiling Bumpass Hell—can be seen during an easy hike along many of the park's 150 miles of hiking trails. The hike from Lassen Park Road to the top of Lassen Peak is only a 5-mile round trip; though it means a 2,000-foot ascent, most hikers make the round-trip trek in less than five hours. From trail's end atop the peak is one of the most spectacular views in the West: the Sierra Nevada, the Coast Range, the Trinity Alps and Lassen's stately, snow-capped sister, Mount Shasta.

Throughout the trail system is vivid evidence that Lassen Volcanic National Park is more than a textbook on volcanism. In this park, destruction and creation exist side by side. At first glance, much of the park reminds the visitor of the moon's surface: a seemingly endless landscape of dullish gray lava beds. Yet throughout the area are lush forests of fir, pine and cedar, crashing waterfalls, a network of jewel-like lakes and quiet meadows. Wildflowers—alpine shooting stars, violets and lilies, to name three—appear in lavish displays after the first snowmelt of spring at lower elevations, later on higher slopes. Some species can be seen until the first snow of the following season. Surprising to some, soil created from disintegrating volcanic ash is very rich, as evidenced by the unusually long blooming season of plants. Botanists number Lassen's wildflower species in the hundreds.

Lassen's lakes—Juniper, Butte and Snag Lakes are the three largest—attract many migratory birds. In fall, bird lovers congregate to count and photograph many waterfowl such as Canadian geese and wood ducks, winging south for the winter. Three species of trout—rainbow, brown and brook—tempt the angler in backcountry lakes, though fishing is considered marginal at Lassen most of the year. Throughout the park are deer, fox and marten; Lassen counts a few bears among its wildlife, but most are shy creatures which prefer backcountry solitude. In any event, they should never be approached.

Getting the best out of an off-season visit to Lassen takes a bit of planning, patience . . . and some plain old luck in the weather department. The Lassen area is cool in summer and cold in winter, with

temperatures dropping dramatically with increasing altitude. The snow season can be long, from October to late May, June or July in some years, and heavy snowpacks of 30 feet or more are not uncommon. After the first snowfall, Lassen Park Road is closed until the spring thaw, except for a short section at the southwestern entrance leading to the Lassen snow sports area. Trails are closed about the same time, except to the few hardy alpine backpackers equipped for heavy winter adventure. Permits for backpacking are required.

Whatever the weather, Lassen can be an exhilarating experience in midwinter, and snow sports such as downhill and cross-country skiing are increasingly popular in the area near Mineral. Interpretive programs are conducted year-round. They add a useful dimension to a Lassen visit in midwinter, though participants then will be wearing snowshoes instead of sneakers.

The "time window" for off-season visiting to Lassen Volcanic National Park is quite narrow. It fluctuates from year to year. This is the period between Labor Day (when peak summer visitation drops off dramatically) to the first snow, and between the spring thaw and the onrush of another summer visitor season. If solitude and silence are important to you but slogging through snowdrifts is not, telephone park headquarters in advance of your visit for the latest weather and driving information.

Lassen Volcanic National Park Mineral, CA 96063, (916) 595-4444
Access: From Red Bluff, 40 miles east via State Hwy. 36. From Redding, 40 miles east via State Hwy. 44. From Susanville, 65 miles west via State Hwy. 36.

Larry Ulrich

Season: Park open all year. Ski and winter sports area (near Mineral) open Thanksgiving to mid-April. Park roads and trails open June through October, limited access at other times. Winter sports area near the southwest entrance.

Visitor Center: At Manzanita Lake (temporary) and southwest entrance.

Lodging: In park: Drakesbad Guest Ranch, (916) 595-3306. Nearby: Mineral, and Hat Creek.

Camping: Four campgrounds with trailer space and full facilities; three campgrounds with limited facilities (no trailers). First come, first served; camping permitted late May to October. One group campground; reservations required (916) 595-4444.

Services: Gas, meals, food and supplies available in the park at Manzanita Lake Camper Service Store and Chalet, and at nearby Mineral and Hat Creek.

Activities: Over 150 miles of hiking trails, backpacking by permit, skiing, swimming, boating, fishing, riding.

For further information on permits, fees, reservations and park regulations, write or call park headquarters.

25

J F M A M J J A S O N D
Lassen Volcanic annual visitors, 440,000

MOUNT LASSEN *hasn't erupted since 1915, but its volcanic furnace is still at work. This is Hot Springs Creek, one of several thermal springs which owe their temperature to the national park's volcanism.*

CALIFORNIA'S LONG CURV-ING SHORE. *California has one of the longest and most varied coastlines in the nation, offering countless opportunities for water-oriented recreation, sightseeing and observing nature. From Mexico to Oregon, the shore extends 850 miles— longer than any state except Alaska. And if you add the edges of all the various bays, tidal rivers, sounds and offshore islands, the actual shoreline distance stretches to an astonishing 3,477 miles, give or take a few feet here and there due to the capricious, erosive nature of wind and wave.*

Along this coast are sheer cliffs and wide, sandy beaches, offshore rocks and forested campgrounds, wave-pounded headlands and quiet coves where signs of man are few.

While some of the California shore is held in private ownership, most of it is accessible to visitors via a fine system of county, state and federal parks and preserves. Five of the 19 National Park System sites in California, in fact, front on the Pacific Ocean, as does a portion of the sixth, Redwood National Park. Many have picnicking, camping and hiking facilities; all except one (Channel Islands National Park) can be reached easily by paved highway, and all offer superb opportunities to observe wildlife and plants that flourish along the eastern edge of the world's largest ocean.

At the southern end of the coast is Cabrillo National Monument, perched atop 420-foot-high Point Loma. The monument, from which migrating gray whales can be seen offshore in winter, commemorates the arrival in 1542 of the Portuguese explorer Juan Rodriguez Cabrillo. Many fine public beaches are north of San Diego on the way to Los

Larry Ulrich

NOYO HARBOR *(top) and the Del Norte County coast are only two places in coastal California where the vacationer can get away from crowds and enjoy tranquil beauty.*

Angeles. Offshore Southern California are eight virtually unpopulated islands of which five—Anacapa, Santa Barbara, San Miguel, Santa Cruz and Santa Rosa—comprise Channel Islands National Park, established in 1980. The park visitor center is in Ventura; boat trips to the park islands are scheduled year around.

At Point Conception north of Santa Barbara, the gale-swept, so-called Cape Horn of North America, both coastline and climate change dramatically. Here is the southern end of storied Big Sur, 90 miles of incomparable shoreline along winding Highway 1. Big Sur merges at its northern end with the equally dramatic shoreline of the Monterey Peninsula, with its miles of white beaches, craggy rocks and gnarled cypresses.

Following the San Francisco northern and western shoreline, the 26,000-acre Golden Gate National Recreation Area is a coastal experience of a different kind, its attractions including Muir Woods, Fort Point near the Golden Gate Bridge, and the former penal colony of Alcatraz.

At Point Reyes National Seashore, an hour's drive north of the Golden Gate, are some of California's finest beaches, sea cliffs, lagoons, wooded ridges and offshore bird and sea lion colonies, all given federal protection in 1962.

From Point Reyes north to Oregon, you are in the heart of the Redwood Empire, a coastline almost devoid of people in the off-season. Here, you'll drive through or past the old Russian fort colony of Fort Ross, the timber country of Mendocino and the sports-fishing mecca of Noyo, a town that time seems to have forgotten. Along the way, accessible from Highway 101, are at least a dozen state beaches and wildlife preserves.

Redwood National Park

Redwood National Park in California was established in 1968 to preserve and protect fast-diminishing forests of earth's tallest trees: the coast redwood (*Sequoia sempervirens*). John Muir called redwoods the "kings of their race"—lofty, sky-reaching monarchs of unforgettable beauty that are living links to the Age of Dinosaurs.

Conifers (cone producers) were the first trees in the Plant Kingdom, and redwoods were the first conifers. Fossil records indicate there were once about 12 or 15 species. After millions of years, however, some of the species died out due to sweeping global climatic changes and to other causes. Today, only three species remain, and two of them are found only in California and a small section of southern Oregon. The giant sequoia, *Sequoiadendron giganteum* is found only in the Sierra Nevada mountain range of eastern California, and the coast redwood prefers a habitat near the western shoreline (the smaller dawn redwood grows naturally only in China).

No other tree in the world is taller than the coast redwood, and few trees live longer. Mature redwoods average 200 to 250 feet in height, are 10 to 15 feet in diameter, and range from 400 to 800 years in age. Many grow both taller and older. A specimen discovered in 1963 on the banks of Redwood Creek measured 367.8 feet tall—the world's tallest tree.

Some coast redwoods are believed to be 2,000 years old, and scientifically speaking, they could grow forever. Resistant to both rot and insects (which almost proved their undoing in the hands of loggers), they usually succumb to fire, lightning or windstorms, rather than age.

Surprisingly, coast redwoods begin life as seeds not much larger than a pinhead, requiring more than 125,000 to weigh a single pound. Nor do they have a taproot; that they manage to survive on a very shallow root system is yet another reason they are so admired.

Coast redwoods grow in a narrow, 450-mile-long coastal strip along the California coast into southern Oregon. Once flourishing north to the Arctic, this is their final retreat, the so-called Redwood Country of seacoast California. Climate in the region is ideal for redwood growth: mild, wet winters, generally dry but foggy summers. Rainfall in Redwood National Park averages 60 to 100 inches per year, but it can total much more. In one year, 174 inches was recorded and in 1964, the rain-swollen Klamath River rose to 90 feet and destroyed a town of the same name.

Summer fog is critical to redwood growth, and these trees could not survive without it. Generated when warm, moist marine air passes over the cold surface of the Pacific, fog replenishes the hundreds of gallons of moisture lost by the trees through evaporation or *transpiration*. Fog drifting silently through the redwood groves enhances a summer visit; "cathedral-like" is the effect many feel as they stand beneath the great trees shrouded in mist.

When it was established in 1968, Redwood National Park included 58,000 acres. An additional 48,000-acre section was authorized in 1978 as peripheral protection for the original park. And that protection was long in coming. Written records of the coast redwood date back to 1769 when a missionary, Friar Juan Crespi, visited the region. He described the trees as "the highest, largest and straightest" he had ever seen, and named them *palo colorado* ("red tree" in Spanish) for the tint of their bark. Later scientists applied the Latin name *Sequoia sempervirens*, the second word of which means "ever green."

Loggers set up operations about 1850 when the species' value as rot-proof, virtually indestructible lumber was discovered. The rush to exploit the trees was on. In 1960, a study was made to determine the extent of a century of logging, and the results were astonishing. From an original 2,000,000 acres of primeval coast redwood forest, only 300,000 acres remained untouched, largely through earlier efforts to establish a system of redwood state parks. The Save-the-Redwoods League had campaigned for federal protection from its founding in 1918; the lobbying at last bore fruit when Congress set aside the national park on the league's 50th birthday.

You'll see thousands of redwoods of various sizes and ages in a visit here. Yet the park is far more than redwoods alone. Within its boundaries are three California state redwoods parks, each with its special points of interest, a spectacular seacoast, a lacework of meadow-like prairies, and a system of rivers, creeks, streams and both freshwater and saltwater lagoons that teem with life.

Heavy rainfall stimulates both plant and animal life. In spring and fall, the park's location on the Pacific Flyway attracts many migrating bird species; in all, birdwatchers have counted more than 350 species within the park. Intertidal invertebrates number nearly 200, and river otters, mink and beavers inhabit many freshwater sections. Rare and endangered species are here, too, including bald eagles, peregrine falcons, brown

27

28

A FOOTBRIDGE *leads across Prairie Creek in Prairie Creek Redwoods State Park (opposite), where hikers may savor the quiet beauty of groves of coast redwoods and associated plants. Named simply Big Tree (left), this redwood, also in Prairie Creek, stands 305 feet tall and has a diameter exceeding 21 feet.*

29

BIG TREE

	FT	MTRS
HEIGHT	305	93.8
DIAMETER	21.3	6.6
CIRCUMFERENCE	67	20.6

Larry Ulrich

pelicans in summer, Aleutian Canada geese and, in season, California gray whales just offshore.

Visitors may also spot black bears, mountain lions, porcupines, coyotes, raccoon, bobcats and—perhaps the most majestic of all—Roosevelt elk. Largest of the park's mammals, elk are seen mostly in coastal sections of the park, and although they may seem tame, they should never be approached.

Except for heavy rains from November to March, Redwood is a national park whose weather encourages visiting any time of year. Spring and fall are ideal times to avoid crowds and the inevitable midsummer traffic along State Hwy. 101 which extends the length of the national and state redwood park system. Redwood ranges in elevation from sea level to 3,097 feet, so no part of it is difficult to reach on foot, though some of the trails in its 150-mile system may wind the inexperienced. Many of the preserved redwood groves can be visited only a short walk from the paved road. Other trails lead to prairie, forest and along the seacoast. For fishermen, Redwood National Park offers both freshwater and marine species: coho and chinook salmon, and rainbow, coast cutthroat and steelhead trout, as well as smelt, silversides perch, herring and flounder in brackish coastal lagoons.

The administering National Park Service maintains no campgrounds of its own within the park. But there are 349 campsites—most of them open all year—available in the three state parks. Reservations are required. The largest, Prairie Creek Redwoods State Park, covers 12,240 acres. It is located north of Orick on Hwy. 101. Its dense forests hold many 300-foot-high, old-growth red-

woods. Gold Bluffs Beach and Fern Canyon, the latter a 50-foot-deep cleft whose sides are blanketed by a delicate, five-fingered species of fern, are also in this park.

Del Norte Coast Redwoods State Park, covering 6,400 acres, borders the Pacific. Rhododendrons and spectacular seascapes are special reasons for a visit here. Del Norte extends south of Jedediah Smith Redwoods State Park to False Klamath Cove.

The 9,200 acres of Jedediah Smith State Park (named for an early explorer) include the 5,000-acre National Tribute Grove of mostly old-growth trees, which honors American fighting men killed in World War II. The park is located along the Smith River, off Hwy. 199, north of Crescent City.

When the crowds have gone, Redwood National Park stages one of the finest shows in nature. As the first frost announces summer's end and the approach of winter, rivers and streams begin to reflect the golden yellows and rusty browns of maples; at the mouth of the Klamath River, silver and king salmon begin wriggling their way upstream to spawn. Autumn is an especially rewarding time for the photographer, but no less so than spring when wildflowers turn meadows into vivid landscapes. Favorites among flowering plants here are the calypso orchid, Indian paintbrush, columbine, and the park's floral "trademark"—the delicate redwood sorrel.

And towering above all are the redwoods.

Redwood National Park 1111 Second Street, Crescent City, CA 95531, (707) 464-6101

Access: From the Oregon coast, south on U.S. Hwy. 101. From Eureka and Arcata, north on U.S. 101. From Grants Pass and Medford, Oregon, east via U.S. Hwy. 199. From Redding, California, east via U.S. Hwy. 299.

Season: Park open all year.

Visitor Center: At Crescent City, Hiouchi ranger station, and Redwood Information Center.

Lodging: In park: none. Nearby: Crescent City, Klamath and Orick.

Camping: In park: Redwood Hostel, 6 miles north of Klamath. Nearby: The three state parks (Jedediah Smith, Del Norte, Prairie Creek) and national forests have campgrounds for tents, campers and trailers up to 26 feet. Primitive camping at Nickel Creek, DeMartin Prairie, Flint Ridge and Redwood Creek. Reservations through Ticketron, or through the Reservation Office, California Dept. of Parks and Recreation, P.O. Box 2390, Sacramento, CA 95811. Reservations are helpful from July 1 through Labor Day. Campsites not filled by reservations available first come, first served.

Activities: Driving, shoreline walks, hiking, horseback riding, swimming, fishing, photography, bird and wildlife watching, field seminars in summer.

For further information on permits, fees, reservations and park regulations, write or call park headquarters.

J F M A M J J A S O N D
Redwood annual visitors, 680,000

Other Selected Sites

CALIFORNIA

Cabrillo National Monument
P.O. Box 6670, San Diego, CA
92106. Telephone (619) 293-5450.
On Point Loma, San Diego.
Memorializes landing in 1542 of
Portuguese explorer Juan Rodri-
guez Cabrillo; gray whale
watching during winter. Site of
Old Point Loma Lighthouse built
in 1854.

Channel Islands National Park
1901 Spinnaker Dr., Ventura, CA
93001. Telephone (805) 644-8262.
Offshore islands of Anacapa,
Santa Barbara, San Miguel, Santa
Cruz and Santa Rosa. Natural
and cultural resources include
Indian middens, sea lion rook-
eries, nesting seabirds, unique
plants and mammals. Camping
and hiking.

**Death Valley National Monu-
ment** Death Valley, CA 92328.
Telephone (619) 786-2331. Southeastern California. Largest
national monument displays
wide variety of desert flora and
fauna, old mining activity, historic Scotty's Castle; contains
lowest point in the United States.
Camping and hiking.

**Devils Postpile National Monu-
ment** Sequoia-Kings Canyon
National Park, Three Rivers, CA
93271. Telephone (209) 565-3341.
Near Minaret Summit, central
California. Columns 40 to 60 feet
high of basalt formed from lava
100,000 years ago. Fishing,
camping, and hiking.

Fort Point National Historic Site
P.O. Box 29333, Presidio of San
Francisco, CA 94129. Telephone
(415) 556-1693. Remains of 19th
Century U.S. Army coastal fort.

**Golden Gate National Recrea-
tion Area** Fort Mason, San
Francisco, CA 94123. Telephone
(415) 556-0560. Follows San Francisco Bay's northern and western
shores. Scenic, recreational and
historic areas and vistas of city
and bay on 26,000-acre coastal
site. Home of the National Mari-
time Museum and its collection of
historic vessels.

Joshua Tree National Monument
74485 National Monument Dr.,
Twentynine Palms, CA 92277.
Telephone (619) 367-7511.
Located 140 miles east of Los
Angeles. Preserves ecosystem of
Mojave and Colorado Deserts,
including the unique Joshua
tree. Camping and hiking.

Lava Beds National Monument
P.O. Box 867, Tulelake, CA

96134. Telephone (916) 667-2282.
Located 93 miles from Klamath
Falls, Oregon. A diverse landscape formed from molten
volcanic lava activity. Relics of
Modoc Indians. Camping and
hiking.

**Muir Woods National Monu-
ment** Mill Valley, CA 94941.
Telephone (415) 388-2595.
Located 17 miles north of San
Francisco. Named for conservationist John Muir, the site
preserves a virgin stand of coastal
redwoods. Hiking.

Pinnacles National Monument
Paicines, CA 95043. Telephone
(408) 389-4578. In central California Coast Range mountains.
Caves and rock formations rising
to 3,300 feet. Camping and
hiking.

Point Reyes National Seashore
Point Reyes, CA 94956. Telephone (415) 663-1092. Located
40–45 miles north of San Francisco. Spectacular beaches, tall
cliffs, lagoons and forested
ridges, noted for offshore birds
and sea lion colonies. Camping
and hiking.

**Santa Monica Mountains
National Recreation Area** Suite
140, 22900 Ventura Blvd., Wood-
land Hills, CA 91364. Telephone
(818) 888-3770. Canyons, streams,
beaches and rolling hills on
50,000 acres of federal, state and
local land. Camping and hiking.

**Whiskeytown-Shasta-Trinity
National Recreation Area** P.O.
Box 188, Whiskeytown, CA
96095. Telephone (916) 241-6584.
Many water-related activities on
Whiskeytown Lake, formed by a
dam; 6,209-foot-high Shasta Bally
peak. Camping and hiking.

31

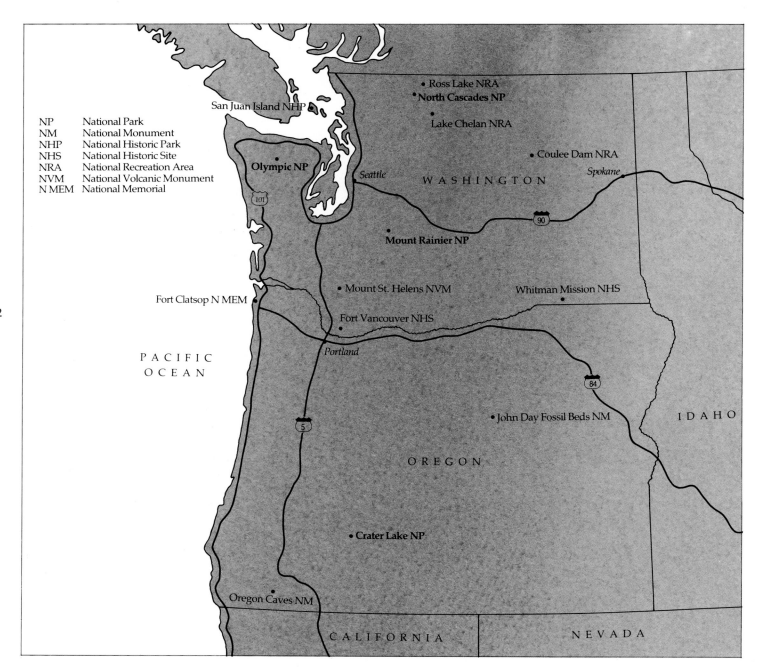

NP National Park
NM National Monument
NHP National Historic Park
NHS National Historic Site
NRA National Recreation Area
NVM National Volcanic Monument
N MEM National Memorial

• Ross Lake NRA
North Cascades NP
• Lake Chelan NRA

• Coulee Dam NRA

San Juan Island NHP

Olympic NP

W A S H I N G T O N

Seattle

Spokane

101

90

Mount Rainier NP

Fort Clatsop N MEM

• Mount St. Helens NVM

Whitman Mission NHS

Fort Vancouver NHS

Portland

P A C I F I C
O C E A N

84

5

• John Day Fossil Beds NM

I D A H O

O R E G O N

• Crater Lake NP

Oregon Caves NM

C A L I F O R N I A

N E V A D A

32

OREGON & WASHINGTON

CRATER LAKE, MOUNT RAINIER, NORTH CASCADES & OLYMPIC NATIONAL PARKS

The story sounds apocryphal but witnesses swear it really happened. Three friends were discussing vacation plans over lunch in a Midwest restaurant. Two were originally from Seattle; the third had never been west of the Rocky Mountains. The latter said he planned to visit the home state of the other two. "I'm going to the Northwest," he said. "You mean the *Pacific* Northwest," one of the others corrected. "That's not quite it, either," put in the third. "He means the *Great* Pacific Northwest!"

Such homegrown pride is understandable when you consider the nature of America's vast, rugged northwest corner, the states of Oregon and Washington. Here is a land of indescribable beauty and diversity, much of it still virtually unspoiled and untouched despite human inroads of the Space Age. If you are an outdoorsman, a seeker of wild, scenic places, the Pacific Northwest speaks for itself in terms of grandeur: un-tamed rivers, beaches fiercely preserved in their natural state, mountain wilderness reached only by hiking trails, dense forests blanketing vast hillsides, quiet, seldom-visited, flower-strewn meadows. Here, too, are remnants of glaciers, ski slopes almost at city outskirts, hundreds of primitive campgrounds, a necklace of snow capped volcanic peaks.

Combined, the land area of Oregon and Washington represents one tenth of the contiguous United States, almost twice the size of New England. Northwesterners are, for the most part, urban dwellers, and yet their total population is less than that of New York City. Much of this area is still undeveloped. Forests alone cover more land than is in all of Kansas, which may explain why the Northwest is one of the country's leading lumber producers, as well as home to 4 of the nation's 49 national parks.

Oregon and Washington are late-bloomers as states go, although they played an important role in westward migration. Oregon did not become a state until 1859; Washington joined the Union 30 years later, in 1889. It was not until World Wars I and II that the Northwest became urbanized and industrialized to any extent, and although airplanes and spacecraft now help fuel the economy, it is still the logger and the commercial fisherman who is king.

Looking down on the Pacific Northwest from space, an astronaut would notice at least six major distinguishing physical features—landforms—of this region, seven if you count the coastline that separates North America from the world's largest ocean.

Dominating all is the mighty north-south mountain range of the Cascades, capped by a string of volcanic peaks which stretches from Mount Garibaldi in British Columbia to northern California. Geologically, the Cascades are young mountains, a highly volatile section of the so-called Ring of Fire, a tectonic perimeter encircling the Pacific which is largely responsible for earthquakes and volcanic eruptions which have shaped the face of the West Coast. The Cascades began to uplift only about seven million years ago—an eyeblink in geologic time—at the juncture of two major sections of the earth's surface, the Pacific Plate and the San Juan de Fuca Plate. About three million years ago, magma—the stuff of which volcanic fury is made—began rising through the earth's crust, and the Cascades were born. Much later, during the Ice Age, glaciers completed the mountain building by whittling and carving the risen mountains and scooping out depressions which later became lakes and valleys.

The Cascades are a place of spectacular beauty, and although modern roads lead to them, there are remote canyons, peaks, valleys, lakes and streams which can be reached only on foot, and which rarely see a human being.

The landscape west of the Cascades is considerably wetter and cooler than that to the east, and it is this varying moisture that determines the type of plant growth on either side of the mountains.

There are an estimated 600 active volcanoes throughout the world today, most of them strung along mountain ranges like the Cascades, where tectonic plates join. "Active" means it is possible that they could erupt at any time, though we usually classify volcanoes as either "active," "dormant" or "extinct."

All three national parks in the Cascades present vivid evidence of both volcanism and glaciation. At 14,410 feet in elevation, Mount Rainier, crown jewel of Mount Rainier National Park, is Washington's highest point, a mountain clad in dense forests of Douglas fir, red cedar and western hemlocks which climb high above mossy, fern-draped valley floors. Rainier has 27 named glaciers—the largest single system in the lower 48 states.

Glaciers are also scattered throughout North Cascades National Park, established in 1968, where Washington and Canada meet. Here are high, ragged peaks, icefalls, waterfalls and alpine splendor. Actually, North Cascades is considered a national park *complex*, since two federally administered national recreation areas—Lake Chelan and Ross Lake—lie within its boundaries.

Crater Lake in southern Oregon is the remnant of a volcano that last erupted between 6,600 and 7,000 years ago. Its namesake lake was formed when the volcano's walls collapsed. There are two especially distinguishing features about this southernmost park of the Northwest: its blueness and its great depth.

The second feature to attract our astronaut's attention is the Columbia River. Wandering 1,200 miles from its headwaters in British Columbia to the Pacific, it is an imposing stream indeed, the only river of the Pacific Northwest which has managed to penetrate the barrier of the Cascade Range on its way to the sea. Many other rivers flow through Oregon and Washington en route to the Pacific, but they originate either on the Cascades' western slopes or in the lower-lying Coast Ranges to the west.

The Columbia is to western America what the Mississippi is to the Midwest and South: a major influence in its region not only geographically, but historically and economically as well. Draining almost 260,000 square miles in seven states, the Columbia now is accessible most of its length by highway. In the past, explorers and settlers had to slog along its banks on foot; as far back as the winter of 1805–06, when members of the Lewis and Clark Expedition camped at its mouth on the Pacific, the Columbia was on its way to becoming one of the major arteries of overland exploration into what later became the Oregon Territory, and, still later, the 33rd and 42nd states of the Union.

East of the Cascades, the Columbia passes through rich farmland, orchards, wheat fields and rangeland—a million acres of former desert made productive by the huge concrete Grand Coulee Dam. Out of the Coulee reclamation project has now been created the water sports mecca of the Coulee Dam National Recreation Area.

In its passage through the Cascades, the river offers still more scenic variety: river valley vistas, fossil caves to explore and exposed lava flows attesting to the Cascades' fiery origin.

If he is looking north as his spacecraft is orbiting from Washington toward the Canadian border along the Pacific, our astronaut would observe two more very obvious features. One is the magnificent Olympic Peninsula, the other a long T-shaped inland sea, one side of the T-curving southward along the peninsula, the other reaching up into Canada. The Olympic Peninsula is a broad thumb of land in which the Olympic Mountains and Olympic National Park form the center. Here are found rugged alpine peaks, icy glaciers, thick forests populated with elk, deer, raccoon and beaver. The peninsula is by far the wettest section of the Pacific Northwest and includes the only temperate rain forest found in North America south of Canada. Olympic is one of only three national parks in the contiguous Western

34

states that has an ocean-facing shoreline (the others are Channel Islands and Redwood, both in California).

The inland sea is actually Puget Sound and the Strait of Juan de Fuca leading into it from the Pacific Ocean. The sound reaches 90 miles from the Pacific to its southern terminus near Tacoma. The other arm of the T runs north inside Vancouver Island in British Columbia.

Puget Sound is one of America's finest waterways, and although its shoreline touches the most urbanized part of the Pacific Northwest, you don't have to drive far from cities like Seattle, Tacoma or Bellingham to find wide open spaces. Stately, 7,965-foot-high Mount Olympus, for instance, is only 63 miles as the bald eagle flies from Seattle's Space Needle, and the San Juan Islands offer 172 choices for camping, beachcombing, hiking or summer clambakes only a ferry ride away from downtown. On San Juan Island, one of the numerous islets, is San Juan Island National Historic Park, operated by the National Park Service. The site commemorates the friendship between the United States, Canada and Great Britain since a boundary dispute briefly soured relations between the three in 1859.

Throughout Puget Sound is evidence of the Pacific Northwest's splendid marriage of mountain and sea. Within sight of lofty peaks like Olympus, commercial fishing boats bustle their way among ocean-going freighters, steamships, ferries and fleets of private craft.

The final two landforms, one east of the Cascades and the other west, are the vast, 80,000-square-mile inland empire of the Columbia Plateau, and Oregon's lush river valleys situated between the Cascades and the Coast Range.

Since Grand Coulee Dam, the plateau has become the Pacific Northwest's breadbasket; once desert, it is now one of North America's leading wheat producers. Farther south, in Oregon, flat plateau country graduates upward into wilderness areas such as the Blue Mountains, where trails lead to camping areas in summer and snow sports areas in winter.

Oregon's western valleys are cut down the middle by Interstate 5, and crossed frequently by rivers meandering to the Pacific. Two major rivers, the Rogue and Umpqua, owe their birth to melting snowpack in the Cascades. Many lesser streams—the Coquille, Smith, Siuslas, Alsea, Yaquina, Siletz, Nestucca and Nehalem—head westward from the Coast Ranges. The Willamette, important in early exploration and settlement, owes one fork to each of the mountain systems.

The Northwest coast offers a spectacular variety of activities, from leisurely beachcombing to seascape photography, and from fishing to tidepool prowling. No two miles of this coastline seem the same, and there are endless miles on which, especially off-season, you'll have shore and sea to yourself. The rugged, often rocky Oregon coast is particularly dramatic when swept by storms, as the history of its shipwrecks will prove. U.S. Hwy. 101 hugs the shore almost the length of Oregon traveling north-south, and most "ports" are those requiring a hazardous trip over a river bar. A toll bridge over the Columbia River at its mouth connects the two states at Astoria; its northern end is near the spot where Meriwether Lewis and William Clark spent the winter during their historic journey of exploration. One of Lewis and Clark's assignments was to find the fabled Northwest Passage, sought futilely by seaborne explorers since the 16th Century. The passage didn't exist, of course; that myth Lewis and Clark exploded forever. But the expedition did turn up reams of data on Indians and the geography of the then unknown territory they moved through on their way to the Pacific. The settlement of Oregon and Washington wasn't far behind.

Although later explorers, settlers, farmers, trappers, loggers, fishermen, missionaries and city-builders arrived in successive waves, the Northwest's Indian heritage has always remained strong, and you'll see a lot of evidence of it on a visit here, especially in place names. Seattle, for instance, is named for Chief Seatlh, an Indian who befriended explorers. Many rivers, mountains, national forests, streets and even ferries are named for Indians or tribes: Spokane, Yakima, Shoshone, Siletz are typical.

Except at higher elevations during winter, weather is seldom a deterrent to off-season travel in the Northwest. The region's climate follows a pattern found almost anywhere along the Pacific Coast except that, being closer to the source of storms, born in the Gulf of Alaska, there is generally more precipitation—rain and snow—than in more southerly latitudes. But Northwest weather can vary dramatically depending upon which side of the mountains one happens to be. In the rain forests of the Olympics, for instance, rainfall averages about 140 inches per year, while only a few miles east, near droughts may persist.

Crater Lake National Park

As he was eating lunch one day in the late 19th Century, a Kansas schoolboy named William Gladstone Steel became fascinated over a feature article in the newspaper the meal came wrapped in. The story described a strange lake in the faraway West. Located in southern Oregon, it was a lake, the article said, of incredible blueness, very deep, surrounded by a mountain wilderness. Steel learned that scientists believed the lake had been formed thousands of years earlier when a fiery volcano, Mount Mazama, exploded with extraordinary violence; when the volcano's walls collapsed, a caldera formed and snowmelt eventually filled the caldera to become the lake.

Steel was determined to see the lake, then called Blue Lake. On August 15, 1885, he found himself standing on the rim of what later became known as Crater Lake, just as have millions of others since its discovery in 1853.

But young Steel wasn't content just to look. The lake, he felt, should be preserved for future visitors to see and enjoy. For 17 years, his fascination unflagging, William Steel waged a one-man campaign to include Crater Lake in the then young National Park System. On May 22, 1902, his wish came true with the establishment of Crater Lake National Park.

Crater Lake, whose surface elevation is 6,176 feet, is in the southern portion of the Cascade mountain range, which extends from British Columbia to Northern California. Scientifically speaking, the volcano that created the caldera and lake is dormant; that is, it is unlikely that it will erupt again. Yet here is a place where the effects of a cataclysmic event are so evident that the park remains a living textbook of volcanism.

Millions of years ago, explosive eruptions built a string of volcanoes along the Cascades. Mount Mazama was one of them. Fearful Indians viewed the fiery mountain with awe and respect; its rumbling, they thought, surely was a result of two gods at war. They were forbidden even to look at the mountain. The legend was passed down from generation to generation but the respect persisted; no mention was made of Mazama or the lake it created when later white explorers came through the area in the mid-19th Century. The mountain's "accidental" discovery was left to a party of gold prospectors, led by John Wesley Hillman. An expedition by the U.S. Geological Survey followed, and this in turn produced the newspaper account which had so fascinated young William Steel.

Crater Lake National Park lies in a region of rolling mountains, volcanic peaks and lush evergreen forests. Although the area is subject to heavy snow from October to June (the surface of the lake seldom freezes), the park is open all year. Only Rim Drive is closed because of winter weather. The unplowed park roads are not useless during the snow season, however; cross-country skiing and other snow activities are both encouraged and popular off-season. Snowmobiling is permitted in one restricted area. One of the most popular cross-country skiing opportunities is a 30-mile ski tour around the lake.

Crater Lake Lodge Company offers a snack bar, gift shop and ski rentals in winter. The lodge itself, a picturesque, massive stone and shingle multistoried hostelry opened in 1915, is closed to overnight guests in the winter months.

When the 33-mile Rim Drive is open, however, it offers an excellent, 360-degree panoramic view of the lake, its main features and the surrounding countryside. A spur road leads to the Pinnacles area. The north entrance road crosses the Pumice Desert; the south road winds above Annie Creek Canyon.

Rim Village, where Crater Lake Lodge is located, is near the southwest corner of the lake. An outlook easily reached from the village offers the visitor arriving from the south his first view of the lake itself, and an opportunity to orient himself for more detailed exploring.

In depth, Crater Lake is 1,932 feet at the maximum, 1,500 feet on the average. It is the deepest lake in the United States, the second deepest in the Western Hemisphere, and the seventh deepest in the world.

The national park covers 183,227 acres; Mount Scott, at 8,926 feet, is the highest point and 8,156-foot-high Hillman Peak is the highest point on the rim. Rim Village is at an elevation of 7,100 feet.

The park has a fine system of foot trails ideal for enjoying the park's plants and wildlife. Cleetwood Trail, 1.1 miles long, leads directly to the lake.

From July through September, rangers explain the park's features on organized hikes; winter interpretive walks are offered between December and May. Narrated, two-hour boat tours are available in the summer, with stops both inside the caldera and at Wizard Island.

Snow should not deter the off-season visitor, however, even the one who is not a skier or snowmobiler. When Crater Lake is blanketed by 15-foot snowdrifts is the time many prefer to visit.

Pat O'Hara

MOST VISITORS *to Crater Lake National Park arrive in summer. What they miss are scenes in the park like this one, taken when the rim was deep under a winter snow. Wizard Island is in the background.*

Crater Lake National Park P.O. Box 7, Crater Lake, OR (503) 594-2211

Access: From Klamath Falls, 54 miles north on U.S. 97 and State Hwy. 62. From Medford, 80 miles north on State Hwy. 62.

Season: Park open all year. The south and west entrance roads on State Hwy. 62 are open all year. The north entrance road and Rim Drive are closed from approximately mid-October to mid-June.

Visitor Center: Rim Village Visitor Center and Steel Center Visitor Center at park headquarters.

Lodging: In park: Crater Lake Lodge, open during summer. Reservations available through Crater Lake Lodge, Inc., Crater Lake, OR 97604, phone (503) 594-2511. Nearby: Medford (80 miles), Klamath Falls (54 miles) and Union Creek and Fort Klamath (30 miles).

Camping: In park: From mid-June to October at Lost Creek on Pinnacles Road and Mazama, 0.3 miles east of Annie Springs entrance.

Services: In park: meals at Crater Lake Lodge and Rim Village. Gas, food and supplies at Rim Village. Nearby: Fort Klamath, Union Creek.

Activities: Driving, hiking, swimming, fishing, restricted snowmobiling, cross-country skiing, snowshoeing, backpacking by permit, photography, plant and wildlife watching, boat trips and interpretive programs.

For further information on permits, fees, reservations and park regulations, write or call park headquarters.

J F M A M J J A S O N D
Crater Lake annual visitors, 405,000

Mount Rainier National Park

Rising 14,410 feet, Mount Rainier is not only Washington's highest mountain, it is also one of the most perfectly formed of all volcanoes in the Cascade Range, a snow-clad sentinel towering over the largest single-peak glacier system in the contiguous United States.

Above the 10,000-foot level, Mount Rainier never loses its mantle of snow. Winter meadows above a mile high sometimes are buried 20 to 30 feet deep. And among the many glaciers that radiate downward from the summit, Emmons Glacier alone is 5 miles long, and 600 feet thick in some places, containing 24 *billion* cubic feet of ice. Scaling Rainier's white-tipped summit is a challenge unmatched in North America, and it is on its slopes that many climbers build stamina and skills for the even loftier Everests elsewhere in the world.

No question about it, winter dominates the seasons in this park, which was established by Congress in 1899. But Mount Rainier National Park does have its other seasons, and a visit here can be scheduled to avoid heavy crowds.

Mount Rainier National Park is very nearly square-shaped, its many features encircling Mount Rainier itself, located just a bit west of center. There are 27 named glaciers in the park, the seven main ones radiating outward on all sides of the peak. Moving clockwise, starting with east-pointing Emmons, they are Cowlitz, Nisqually, Tahoma, Puyallup, Carbon, and Winthrop. Should you climb to Columbia Crest at the top of Rainier, you'll be hiking either on or very near one of these massive ice blocks left over from the last Ice Age.

There are six entrances leading to the park's interior. The east and west sides of the park are connected by roads that lead from deep forest into open meadow and then back into forest again. Almost all the way there is a view of Mount Rainier from a different angle. A second through-park road runs north to south along the eastern edge. Except for the road leading from the park's Nisqually entrance to Longmire—location of park headquarters—and Paradise, all roads are closed after the first snow. Even the road to Paradise is sometimes closed briefly during and after storms. Anytime in winter, tire chains should be carried. Sometimes they are mandatory. Auto touring can be a spectacular experience.

Snow sports activities center at Paradise, located at 5,400-foot elevation 13 miles past Longmire. There is excellent cross-country skiing; instruction, equipment rentals and snacks are available here. On midwinter weekends and holidays, the Paradise resort can be jammed with snowshoers, cross-country skiers, and youngsters sliding down the hills on inner tubes.

There is an extensive trail system throughout the park, varying in degree of length and difficulty. Trails range from a 3-mile (round trip) Pinnacle Peak Trail to the Wonderland Trail, a 93-mile route which encircles Mount Rainier.

An especially rewarding hike is the 6-mile Paradise Glacier Trail, starting just west of the Paradise ranger station. Wildflowers are seen just past the trailhead and at Mazama Ridge, one of Mount Rainier's many lava flows. The jagged mountains of the Tatoosh Range rise to the south.

From 6,400-foot-high Sunrise area northeast of Mount Rainier, the highest point in the park accessible by car, there are many trails leading toward the

38

mountain and its glaciers.

A climb to the summit—Columbia Crest—takes two days. Climbers must first register with a park ranger and check in and check out. For the less experienced, techniques are taught in a pre-climb session. Climbers stay overnight at the 10,000-foot level. Shorter guided hikes along Rainier's lower slopes are also available.

Mount Rainier is not only one of the highest volcanoes in the United States, it is also one of the largest. A young mountain by geologic time measurement, it probably started growing hundreds of thousands of years ago from a vent in the earth through which lava flowed outward and downward. Rainier is a dormant volcano; although it has not erupted in this century, at least 14 eruptions occurred in the 19th Century, their fiery debris sometimes blanketing thousands of square miles.

Around the mountain is a series of lesser mountain peaks, lesser in the sense that they are lower and smaller than Rainier, not in terms of their beauty and disruptive potential; Mount St. Helens is less than 40 miles from Rainier.

Changes in the park's plant communities are evident as the hiker climbs from flower-filled mountain meadow toward the summit where there is little but ice, rock and sky. Douglas fir, western red cedar, western hemlock, and lodgepole pine dominate lower slopes, while mountain hemlock and whitebark pine forest slopes between 5,000 and 6,500 feet. More than 700 plant species have been identified in Rainier, as well as 157 species of birds. Common mammals include elk, mountain goat, blacktail deer, black bear, raccoon, mountain lion, beaver, squirrels and chipmunks.

Rainier draws the fisherman, too, but wise is the angler here who heeds the seasons. Several streams provide Eastern brook, rainbow and cutthroat trout. The best time to fish for them is when the snowmelt is low. At other times, glacial silt can turn streams milky, and fishing may be disappointing.

There are five campgrounds with 500 sites in the park, but only Sunshine Point Campground, near Nisqually, is open year around. Camping is also available in national forests which adjoin the park.

In recent years, Rainier has become one of the most popular of all western national parks, drawing up to two million visitors a year. About 70 percent of them come during the peak period of June to September, less than 10 percent from December to March, despite the growing popularity of snow-related activity. In late fall or early spring you'll have many parts of the park almost to yourself, especially those off the beaten track and away from Paradise where most visitors gather. The park as a whole covers 235,404 acres of mountains, hillsides, meadows, valleys, forests and streams.

Mount Rainier National Park Tahoma Woods, Star Route, Ashford, WA 98304, (206) 569-2211
Access: From Tacoma, 70 miles southeast on State Hwy. 410. From Yakima, 103 miles west on U.S. 12.
Season: Park open all year. Snow closes some roads from late November through June. Chains may be required.
Visitor Center: Longmire and Paradise are open all year. Sunrise and Ohanapecosh are open in summer only.
Lodging: In park: National Park Inn at Longmire (year-round). Paradise Inn

(early June-early October). For reservations write or call Mount Rainier Guest Service, Star Route, Ashford, WA 98304, (206) 569-2275. Nearby: Ashford on Hwy. 706 and Alder and Elbe on Hwy. 7 immediately adjacent to the park.
Camping: In park: from June to October at Cougar Rock (8 miles northeast of Nisqually entrance). From May to October at Ipsut Creek (5 miles east of Carbon River entrance) and Ohanapecosh (1½ miles east of Nisqually entrance). From July–September at Whiteriver (5 miles west of White River entrance).
Services: In park: meals at Longmire, Paradise Inn, Paradise Visitor Center and Sunrise. Food and supplies at Longmire and Sunrise. Nearby: meals, gas, food and supplies at Ashford, Elbe, Packwood and Enumclaw.
Activities: Driving, hiking, backpacking by permit, mountain climbing, fishing, snowshoeing, cross-country skiing, snowmobiling, photography, plant and wildlife watching, and interpretive programs.

For further information on permits, fees, reservations and park regulations, write or call park headquarters.

39

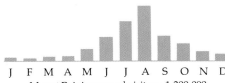

J F M A M J J A S O N D
Mount Rainier annual visitors, 1,300,000

Pat O'Hara

RISING 14,410 FEET *into the Washington sky, Mount Rainier reaches high to disturb waves of moist marine air flowing eastward from the Pacific. It is a superb crown jewel for its namesake national park. The mountain on these pages is mirrored in Reflection Lake. Other typical sights in the park that will awe visitors include, clockwise from above: vine maples at Falls Creek, yellow monkeyflowers (a spring spectacular) at Snow Lake Inlet, some of the glaciers spreading*

Pat O'Hara

outward from Mount Rainier's peak and Comet Falls, one of many waterfalls in the park. There are 27 named glaciers in Mount Rainier's 35-square-mile glacial system, and they are responsible for much of the spectacle that the park represents. Deep valleys separated by high, craggy ridges and broad plateaus found in places like Sunrise—these are features owed to the giant sculptors of the Ice Age. The wildflower show depends upon both elevation and time of year, the blooms occurring earlier in lower meadows and then moving upward as summer nears.

41

Pat O'Hara

Pat O'Hara

GLACIERS: SCULPTORS OF THE ICE AGE. *Almost anywhere you travel in the Western region covered by this book, you'll find evidence of the huge, white natural bulldozers that shaped this land millions of years ago, and which, to some extent, they are ponderously shaping even today.*

They are the glaciers—nature's frozen rivers.

Simply defined, a glacier is heavily packed land ice that is moving because of its great weight and the pull of gravity. That may not be much; some glaciers move only at about the rate of one yard per month. But move they do, sculpting the landscape beneath and behind them as they inch along, just as glaciers have done for millennia.

In the contiguous United States, there are about 800 glaciers altogether, covering a total of about 160 square miles. You'll see examples of their landforming work in all 11 states covered by this book, and you'll see living glaciers in all but Arizona and New Mexico.

Glaciers are not mere adornments of nature; they are useful in many ways. In summer, for instance, about 15 percent of the flow of the Columbia River comes from glacial melt originating in Canada. In places like Tacoma, Washington, and Boulder, Colorado, water from melting glaciers which flows in streams is tapped both for hydroelectric power and as a freshwater supply. According to the U.S. Geo-

Pat O'Hara

THE PEAK OF *Mount Rainier in Washington (below) is typical of places in the West where glaciers may be found. The valleys above Nevada and Vernal Falls in Yosemite National Park (above) are typical of the "hanging valleys" carved by glaciers of the Ice Age.*

logical Survey, three fourths of all the world's freshwater supply is frozen in glaciers large and small.

North Cascades National Park Complex alone includes 318 glaciers—almost half the total in the continental United States. In Mount Rainier National Park, there are 27 named glaciers, covering 35 square miles. Other national parks in the mountainous West have glaciers of their own, all worth seeing, photographing and learning more about.

Some scientists believe that millions of years ago, up to one third of the earth's surface was covered by glacial ice. At one time, a huge continental ice sheet blanketed much of North America, extending as far south as present-day Washington, Idaho and Montana. As global climate alternately cooled and warmed, the glaciers advanced and retreated, grinding away at the land beneath them.

Although we often refer to "the" Ice Age, there were actually several, the last one ending between 10,000 and 12,000 years ago.

In the wake of the Ice Age giants, you'll clearly see their handiwork in many Western national parks: moraines, cirques, U-shaped valleys and lakes which have formed in glacial depressions. "Hanging valleys"—side valleys formed where a small tributary glacier flowed into a main one—are another glacial product. The valley from which 2,425-foot-high Yosemite Falls tumbles is one of the best examples.

42

North Cascades National Park Service Complex

Less than a 2-hour drive from a metropolitan area of nearly two million people lies one of America's great remaining, almost impenetrable wildernesses—the 1,053-square-mile North Cascades National Park Service Complex in north-central Washington State. It is wilderness, yet, perhaps surprisingly, it's also a place where you can ski, go snowmobiling or boating, ride horseback or raft a river, eat a meal or buy a roll of film.

An incomparable region of high, ragged, snow-clad mountain peaks, many glaciers and magnificent lakes, canyons ribboned by waterfalls, meadows blanketed with wildflowers, and a profusion of wildlife, North Cascades is an unusual park in many ways. It is designated a "complex" because it encompasses two national recreation areas—Ross Lake and Lake Chelan—as well as the national park itself. Parts of North Cascades are wilderness. Except for one, short, little-traveled spur road which leads to a point near scenic, 5,684-foot-high Cascade Pass near the southern end, there is not a single vehicular artery anywhere in the two huge tracts of land which make up the park. State Route 20—the northern route across Washington, completed in 1972—meanders through either national forest or one of two national recreation areas. Otherwise, North Cascades is almost entirely a park for the hiker, backpacker, horseback rider and mountaineer. From the south, through the Lake Chelan National Recreation Area, one must either fly, hike, ride a horse or boat to get in.

Doubtless, there are parts of North Cascades that have never felt a human footstep, isolated pockets whose wildlife has never seen—or been seen by—a human. Yet by contrast, recreation and service functions share a peaceful coexistence with the wilderness.

What seems more surprising is that, despite all it has to offer, North Cascades has so few visitors compared to many other national parks its size or even smaller. In one recent year, they totaled only about 685,000—roughly one third the number that visited Yellowstone.

North Cascades is surrounded on three sides by three national forests and on the north by provincial lands of Canada. It is magnificent mountain country. Some have compared its landscape to the Alps of Europe, but with better weather, more diverse forests and a wider variety of wildlife. Seen from a distance, mountain peaks and glaciers dominate. Many of the summits, towering 7,000 to 9,000 feet, were carved in past eons into steep, jagged shapes.

More than 127 alpine lakes lie in glacier-carved, U-shaped valleys where rainbow, Dolly Varden, brook and golden trout await the angler. Most of the lakes are accessible along some of the 360 miles of trail found in the park.

Plant life varies throughout the park depending upon location and altitude. There are examples here of rain forest, alpine tundra, pine forest, high meadow and dry shrubland. Among mammals, you might see a flying squirrel during your visit; more likely you will encounter marmot, chipmunk, beaver, muskrat, porcupine, fox, coyote, black bear, deer and mountain goat.

North Cascades has 318 glaciers, more than half of all those found in the contiguous 48 states. None is accessible directly by road, but you'll see them from almost anywhere in the park.

The park was established in 1968, decades after Yellowstone. However, proposals for the creation of a North Cascades National Park date back almost to the turn of the century.

Nowhere in America are there mountains which present, as surveyor Henry Custer observed in the 19th Century, "such strange, fantastic, dauntless and startling outlines." Even today visitors may be occasionally startled by the rumble of a glacial icefall crashing downward, one of the few sounds to shatter the hush around them.

At Cascade Pass, approached by the only road in the national park, you are afforded one of the best vistas of the rock ridges, glaciers, snowfields, cascading waterfalls and other features of the high country, as well as a bird's-eye view of the Cascade and Stehekin Valleys below. The pass is one of the best routes to follow through the park on foot. A wide, well-maintained, gradual trail originally used by Indians as a trade route, it affords spectacular views of 8,200-foot-high Johannesburg Mountain and its glaciers to the west and, to the east, of river waters rushing toward Lake Chelan.

The lake is one of the natural wonders of North Cascades. Often compared to Switzerland's Lake Lucerne, Chelan is, with a depth of 1,500 feet, one of America's deepest lakes.

The community of Stehekin, at the north end of the lake, is a popular summer destination for visitors, although it can only be reached by floatplane, boat or by trail. A shuttle van operates out of Stehekin three times daily in summer on tours of the park and the Lake Chelan National Recreation Area. Once a prosperous but short-lived fur trading center,

43

the community is surrounded by magnificent wilderness and towering mountains and retains much of its historic charm. A favorite time for many visitors is autumn, when the Stehekin Valley and Washington Pass almost explode with the color of western larch on hillsides nearby. Somewhat of a rarity in the tree world, the larch is one of the few deciduous conifers. It resembles the ponderosa pine in some ways with its great height and straight trunk. In fall, its needles turn bright gold.

The second national recreation area—Ross Lake—extends in a broad swath from southwest to northeast, dividing the two huge parts of the national park. Unlike Lake Chelan, Ross Lake and Diablo Lakes are man-made, formed when the Skagit River was dammed to provide hydroelectric power for the greater Seattle complex. Encompassing 107,000 acres, Ross Lake National Recreation Area is a wildly scenic corridor leading over the Cascade Range. It provides most of the park's campgrounds, recreation facilities and other visitor amenities. Trailheads leading to the wilderness interior of the park originate here, and Cascades Highway, extending down the center of the corridor, is a thoroughly worthwhile scenic drive. Only the western portion of the road is open in winter, however; snow cover and the danger of avalanches forces closing of the eastern part—designated a National Scenic Highway—about mid-November.

From December to mid-February, visitors arriving from the west may see bald eagles feeding on salmon in the Skagit River, one of the most spectacular natural dramas seen in the park. The best place for viewing is the section of highway from Rockport (outside the park) to

44

Pat O'Hara

THIS COLORFUL *display of mountain ash is typical of autumn tree color in North Cascades National Park, Washington. On opposite page: (top) hikers near Ross Lake, (bottom) the rugged Cascade Pass.*

Pat O'Hara

Pat O'Hara

Newhalem. The eagles should not be approached or molested.

Weather is a limiting factor in a visit to North Cascades National Park. But if you prepare adequately for it, no time of year is a poor time to go. Annual rainfall on western slopes can total more than 110 inches (on eastern slopes, perhaps only 34) and the park has recorded as much as 510 inches of snow in a single season. Hypothermia (rapid loss of body heat) is a constant danger even in summer at higher elevations.

Properly prepared, however, and heeding the rangers' friendly advice, a trip to North Cascades is one that will live long in memory.

North Cascades National Park Service Complex 2105 Highway 20, Sedro Woolley, WA 98284, (206) 856-5700

Access: From Burlington on the west and Twisp on the east, follow State Hwy. 20. Hiking access at the northwest corner from State Hwy. 542 east from Bellingham. Access to the Lake Chelan National Recreation Area is by boat, floatplane or trail from Chelan on U.S. 97. Vehicle access to Ross Lake is on an unimproved road from Canada. From Chelan, a privately operated boat is available for the 55-mile trip to Stehekin.

Season: Park open all year.

Visitor Center: Park headquarters at 2105 Highway 20, Sedro Woolley, near State Hwy. 20, 45 miles west of park entrance. There are ranger stations at Marblemount on Hwy. 20, 4 miles west of the park entrance, and at Stehekin.

Lodging: North Cascades Lodge, Stehekin, WA 98852, (509) 682-4711; Diablo Lake Resort, P.O. Box 176, Rockport, WA 98283, phone (206) operator Newhalem 5578, and Ross Lake Resort, Rock-

45

port, WA 98283, phone (206) operator Newhalem 7735. Other accommodations in nearby Chelan, Marblemount and Concrete.

Camping: Campgrounds on first-come, first-served basis. Group campgrounds available by mail reservation. Backcountry and free-trail camping by permit only. All within five miles of Stehekin. Ross Lake NRA has 25 campgrounds; most have limited facilities but all have toilet facilities. Two are open year around, with access from State Hwy. 20. Three others open from April–October with access off Hwy. 20, and one off Canada 3. Other Ross Lake campgrounds are open June 1–November 1 and are accessible by boat or trail only. There are three Diablo Lake campgrounds open May 1–November 1, also accessible by boat only.

Services: Meals served at North Cascades Lodge and Diablo Lake Resort. Food and supplies available at North Cascades Lodge, Diablo Lake, Chelan, Marblemount, Newhalem and Concrete.

Activities: Motor touring, mountain climbing, backpacking by permit, horseback riding, boating, fishing, hunting (in NRA only), commercial river rafting, photography, wildlife and bird watching, interpretive programs.

For further information on permits, fees, reservations and park regulations, write or call park headquarters.

North Cascades annual visitors, 685,000

Olympic National Park

Olympic National Park is the wilderness centerpiece of the wet, wild, scenic Olympic Peninsula in northwest Washington state. Originally established as an elk refuge, upgraded by Congress in 1938 to national park status, it is a dramatic marriage of mountain and sea, and a testimonial to the power and effect of water: wind-driven surf, glacial ice, torrential rainfall, tumbling waterfalls, roaring rivers, heavy snowfall. The park covers nearly 900,000 acres of mountain, meadow, seacoast and forest. Combined with nearly 90,000 additional acres of primitive land in three sections of the Olympic National Forest, the park presents the largest bloc of true wilderness in the United States outside Alaska. Here is a hiker's, camper's, backpacker's, mountaineer's park. But it is also a place whose major features can be seen and appreciated by the auto-bound visitor. To preserve its virgin beauty and to protect its resources, however, no road runs completely through its expanse, and the most enjoyable visit, as is true in most national parks, is on foot.

U.S. Hwy. 101 loops almost entirely around the park, with numerous spur roads leading from coastal communities like Port Angeles to Olympic's rain forests, the high country, valleys and the 57-mile seacoast section, which is the longest remaining primitive shoreline in the contiguous United States. Presiding over all this sprawling, almost undisturbed landscape is stately, snow-clad Mount Olympus, reaching 7,965 feet into the sky, whose slopes hold several of the more than 60 glaciers in the park.

Whatever the time of year, the visitor preparing for a vacation on the Olympic Peninsula would do well to pack a rain-coat topmost in his suitcase. It is wet here, *very* wet. Recording an average of 140 inches of rainfall annually, the peninsula is officially the wettest place in the continental United States; curiously, Sequim (pronounced *Squim*), on the east side of the Olympic Mountains only 30 miles from the park's lush, wet, life-giving rain forests, is the *driest* region of the coastal western United States north of Southern California. In some years, Sequim is fortunate to receive 17 inches of rainfall, a credit to the storm-dispersing power of the rugged mountain range that separates the east side of the peninsula from the west. Rain can occur at any time of year on the Olympic Peninsula, although it is heaviest (about 75 percent) from October through March. Year around, temperatures at sea level are mild, ranging from an average of about 70 degrees F in summer to 40 degrees in winter. Higher elevations of course are colder in both seasons, and snowfall in Olympic National Park rivals rainfall in meteorological record books. Up to 40 feet has been recorded in some years.

The park is open all year, and it is its heavy precipitation that stimulates Olympic plant growth to dimensions (for any given species) found in no other U.S. national park. Here, for instance, will be found red cedar 21 feet thick, Sitka spruce over 13 feet, Douglas fir more than 14 feet across and 300 feet high—all giants of their species, exceeded in diameter and height only by the redwoods of California.

The visitor to the Olympic rain forest may be first impressed with color. Trees seem to drip with a mossy, fernlike, green coating, even fallen trees whose own life has long since expired. Under the forest canopy, the light has a green-

46

MOODY VISTAS *like this one—viewing a cloud bank from Blue Mountain— greet the visitor at nearly every turn in Olympic National Park, Washington.*

Pat O'Hara

ish tint; some say even the rain forest sky is a lush emerald color.

Rain forests are best exemplified in western valleys of the Olympics. Peaks and crags of the mountains wring out most of the moisture carried eastward in Pacific-spawned storm clouds before they can reach eastern slopes. Sitka spruce and western hemlock dominate the forests, but Douglas fir and western red cedar are also common. Near forest streams are stands of bigleaf maple, vine maple, red alder and cottonwood. Mosses carpet the forest floor.

Visitor centers at Port Angeles, Hurricane Ridge and the Hoh Rain Forest, open all year, and at Kalaloch, open only in summer, are the best places for a first-impression look at this national park. Extending south from the park entrance at Port Angeles is a 17-mile road to Hurricane Ridge, paved and kept open most of the winter on weekends. Hurricane Ridge affords one of the best panoramic views of major park features, of the Strait of Juan de Fuca, the San Juan Islands and, in the distance, Mount Olympus' twin sisters, Mount Baker and Glacier Peak. In winter, Hurricane Ridge offers fine snow play opportunities.

The Hoh Rain Forest is reached by a short nature trail past the end of the spur road leading east from Hwy. 101 on the west side of the park. A longer trail—one of 600 miles of footpath throughout the park—extends from this point 9.2 miles to Olympus on the north slope of its namesake peak.

Olympic abounds in bird and animal species. More than 130 kinds of birds have been listed, ranging from great blue herons, geese, swans and many ducks to grouse, woodpeckers, swallows, chickadees and bald eagles. There are an esti-

47

Pat O'Hara

WATER IN ITS MANY FORMS *is the heartbeat of Olympic National Park and the Olympic Peninsula. In the form of snow, it creates a dramatic early winter landscape as in this scene looking toward the Needles Peaks. At the top of these pages, left to right: a camper's tent at the edge of Lena Lake; vine maples and moss in the Hoh Rain Forest; the saltwater wilderness of South Beach; a waterfall, the product of rainfall and snowmelt fed into a mountain stream. Mount*

Pat O'Hara

Pat O'Hara

Olympus in the park is the wettest spot in the continental United States, receiving about 200 inches of precipitation per year. Rains in Olympic may last for days, any time of year, with three-fourths of it falling from October through March. Some of the downward-flowing water is represented by meltwater from the park's nearly 60 glaciers. Whether held in glacial lakes or flowing toward the Pacific, water sets the mood for the Olympic visitor. And that mood can vary greatly, from the crash of surf on the ocean shore to the placid stillness of lake and forest.

Pat O'Hara

mated 56 species of mammals. The largest is the Roosevelt elk, named for President Theodore Roosevelt, the ardent conservationist who designated the site as a national monument in 1909.

For the fisherman, there are more than 100 lakes in Olympic National Park, 2 of them—Crescent Lake and Lake Ozette—more than 10 miles long. There are many streams, large and small. No state license is required to fish for cutthroat, rainbow, brook and Dolly Varden which attract many of the anglers, but a state "punchcard" is needed for steelhead. Rainbow and brook trout are found in some of the lakes; the other species are mostly in streams. Many saltwater species can be caught on the coast.

Olympic's snow season is long, but wildflowers begin to bloom in the meadows long before the first melt in the high country. Glacier lilies persistently push up through the snow, and as soon as the weather begins to warm in spring, lupine, valerian, bistort, hellebore and buttercup add their explosion of purple, white, red and yellow. Rhododendron, salal, swordfern and huckleberry are among the forest understory.

Camping? Take your pick of meadow, lowland forest or primitive beach. There are nearly 1,000 campsites in the park, another 356 in the nearby national forest. Those at lower elevations are open all year; at high elevations, most are closed by snow from about early November to late June or early July. Both boating and swimming are popular during the summer in Crescent Lake and Lake Ozette.

The other face of this amazing park is its 57-mile boundary bordering the Pacific Ocean. Although much of it is inaccessible by automobile, there are many trails, and views from the road at La Push (at the mouth of the Quileute River) and south of Oil City are excellent.

Strolling these lonely beaches, one sees many of the more than 870 islands large and small which lie off the Washington seacoast from Cape Flattery to Copalis Beach, halfway downstate toward Oregon. They are part of the Washington Islands National Wildlife Refuge, now within the park's boundaries. None can be visited, but the populations of seabirds they protect are visible from the coastal park. On the coast, too, are piles of driftwood heaped up by storms which may have originated in Asia, and communities of literally thousands of flora and fauna uncovered by tides of the restless Pacific Ocean.

Olympic National Park 600 East Park Ave., Port Angeles, WA 98362, (206) 452-4501, Ext. 230

Access: The park is encircled by U.S. Hwy. 101. Several entrances on the perimeter.

Season: Park open all year. High-elevation roads and trails are normally open June 1 to October 1.

Visitor Center: Port Angeles and Hoh Rain Forest are open all year. Kalaloch Visitor Center open only in summer.

Lodging: Reservations may be made for in-park lodging at Kalaloch Lodge, Inc., HC80, Box 1100, Forks, WA 98331, (206) 962-2271; Log Cabin Resort, 6540 E. Beach Rd., Port Angeles, WA 90362, (206) 928-3245; Lake Crescent Lodge, HC62, Box 11, Port Angeles, WA 98362, (206) 928-3211. Nearby accommodations: Port Angeles, Aberdeen, Forks, Sequim and Shelton. For reservations, write Olympic Peninsula Resort & Hotel Assn., Coleman Ferry Terminal, Seattle, WA 98104.

Camping: There are 18 campgrounds throughout the park. Ten have full facilities, eight have limited facilities. Group reservations can be made at Kalaloch, Mora or Ozette Ranger Stations. All others, first come, first served.

Services: Meals served at Hurricane Ridge, Fairholm, Kalaloch and Lake Crescent. Food and supplies obtainable in the park at some lodges. Nearby: Sequim, Port Angeles, Forks, Shelton and Aberdeen.

Activities: Driving, hiking, mountain climbing, backpacking by permit, horseback riding, boating, canoeing, kayaking, fishing, swimming, skiing, snowshoeing, wildlife watching, photography, interpretive programs.

For further information on permits, fees, reservations and park regulations, write or call park headquarters.

J F M A M J J A S O N D
Olympic annual visitors, 2,945,000

Other Selected Sites

OREGON

Fort Clatsop National Memorial Route 3, Box 604-FC, Astoria, OR 97103. Telephone (503) 861-2471. Six miles south of Astoria on U.S. 101. Site of encampment of Lewis and Clark Expedition in winter of 1805/6.

John Day Fossil Beds National Monument 420 West Main St., John Day, OR 97845. Telephone (503) 575-0721. In John Day. Five epochs of plant and animal fossils are preserved and displayed. Hiking.

Oregon Caves National Monument 19000 Caves Hwy., Cave Junction, OR 97523. Telephone (503) 592-2100. Located 20 miles south of Cave Junction on Oregon Hwy. 46. Caves and intricate flowstone formations formed by groundwater dissolving bedrock. Hiking.

WASHINGTON

Coulee Dam National Recreation Area P.O. Box 37, Coulee Dam, WA 99116. Telephone (509) 633-1360, ext. 441. Northeast Washington. Franklin D. Roosevelt Lake, 150 miles long, formed by Grand Coulee Dam; camping, hiking, fishing and many other water-related recreational activities.

Fort Vancouver National Historic Site 1501 East Evergreen Blvd., Vancouver, WA 98661. Telephone (206) 696-7655. Near Vancouver. Preserved remains of a U.S. Army post and Hudson's Bay Company trading post established in 1849.

Lake Chelan National Recreation Area (See North Cascades

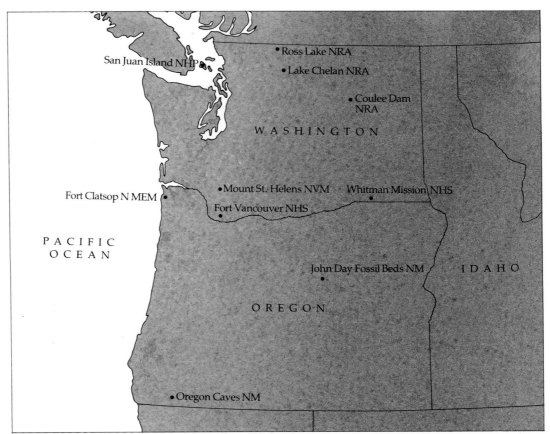

National Park Complex.)

Mount St. Helens National Volcanic Monument 3029 Spirit Lake Highway, Castle Rock, WA 98611. Telephone (206) 274-6644. Visitor Center on State Hwy. 504, west of Interstate 5, 50 miles north of Portland, Oregon. Open all year, the Visitor Center has exhibits interpreting the eruption of Mount St. Helens in 1980. Private and U.S. National Forest camping and hiking available except in winter near the volcano itself.

Ross Lake National Recreation Area (See North Cascades National Park Complex.)

San Juan Island National Historic Park Box 429, Friday Harbor, WA 98250. Telephone (206) 378-2240. Reached by ferry from Anacortes, Washington, 83 miles north of Seattle. Commemorates peaceful relations between the United States, Great Britain and Canada, including Canadian and American military campsites. Hiking.

Whitman Mission National Historic Site Route 2, Box 247, Walla Walla, WA 99362. Telephone (509) 522-6360. Seven miles west of Walla Walla on U.S. 12. A landmark on the Oregon Trail, mission was established by Dr. and Mrs. Marcus Whitman, slain by Indians in 1847.

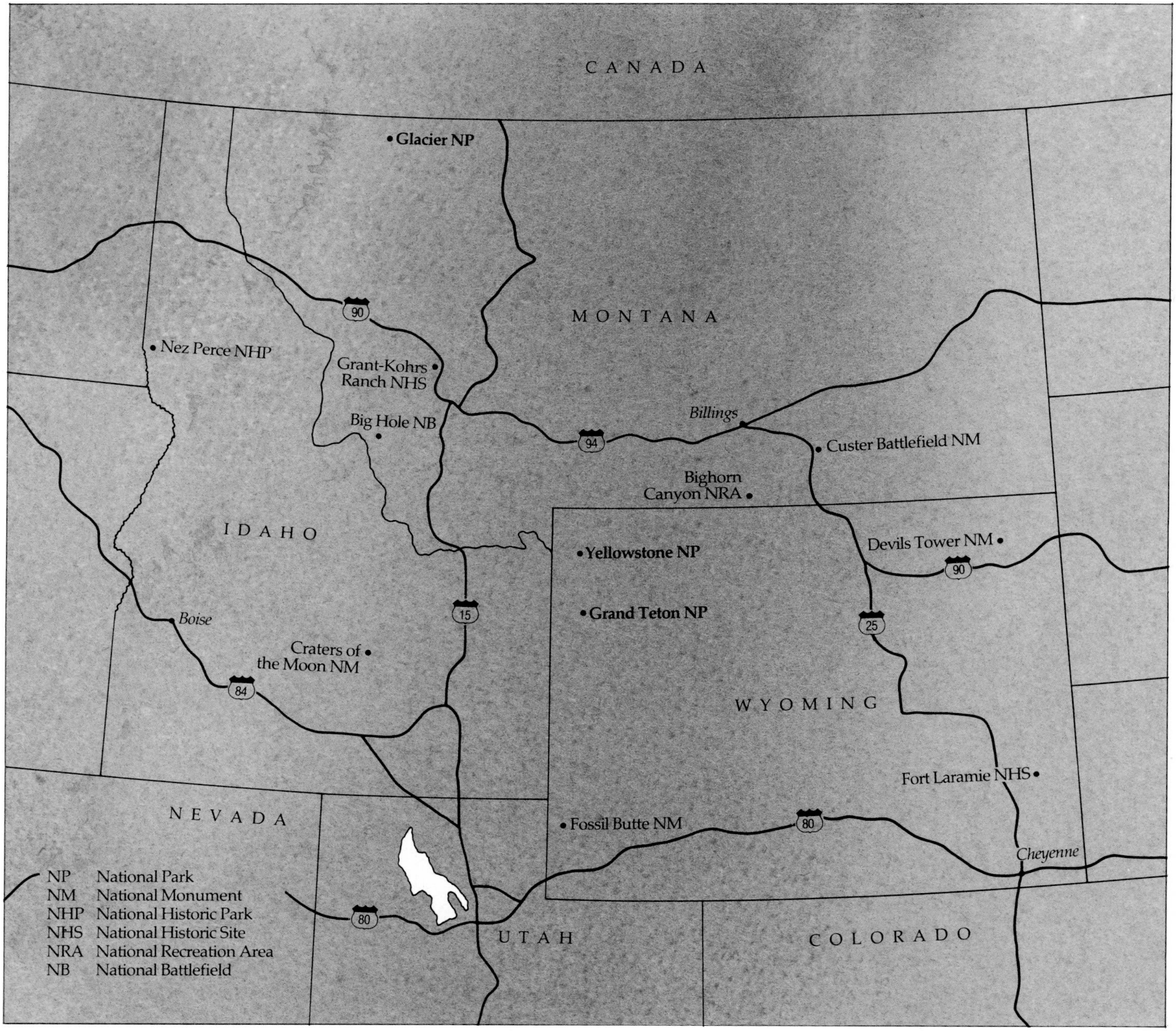

CANADA

• Glacier NP

MONTANA

90

• Nez Perce NHP

Grant-Kohrs •
Ranch NHS

Big Hole NB •

94

Billings

• Custer Battlefield NM

Bighorn
Canyon NRA •

IDAHO

• Yellowstone NP

Devils Tower NM •

90

Boise

15

• Grand Teton NP

25

Craters of •
the Moon NM

WYOMING

84

NEVADA

Fort Laramie NHS •

• Fossil Butte NM

80

80

Cheyenne

NP   National Park
NM   National Monument
NHP   National Historic Park
NHS   National Historic Site
NRA   National Recreation Area
NB   National Battlefield

UTAH

COLORADO

IDAHO, MONTANA & WYOMING
GLACIER, YELLOWSTONE & GRAND TETON NATIONAL PARKS

When author John Gunther made a swing around the American West in 1951 to update his best-selling book, *Inside USA,* he found, not to his surprise, that most areas were in need of drastic information overhauling. In less than a decade since Gunther had first visited, much of the data he had collected was woefully outdated. In terms of population, budget and gross product, California had become a mini-nation. Mile-high, postwar Denver had exploded with growth. Phoenix, which only a century earlier was a remote desert oasis, had become the country's fastest-growing city. Almost every page of his book, Gunther found, was growing stale almost by the hour. But there was one exception, and it was an exception that would apply even today: the three Rocky Mountain states of Idaho, Wyoming and Montana, which a later historian lumped together as the Mountain North of Western America.

A vast, sometimes lonely, thinly populated region dominated by the northern Rockies, the Mountain North was and remains a passive, pleasant antidote to the busier, noisier, bustling West of the Pacific Coast states. It's a land of wide open spaces under a wide open sky, of rolling plains and rugged mountains, of millions of acres of unhurried wilderness and woodlands where deer, elk and antelope roam almost unmindful of people. The cowboys, miners, Indians and ranchers you'll meet here aren't refugees from a Hollywood film set or plants of the local chamber of commerce. True to life, they have been mainstays of the economy here for many generations.

"Thinly populated" is somewhat misleading; "underpopulated" would be more accurate. Despite the size of the three states (Montana, the largest, is bigger than Japan; even Idaho, the smallest, could swallow up two Scotlands), the Mountain North supports barely more than 2.2 million human souls. And it means an average population density of only about six people for each of the three states' combined 324,764 square miles—only one tenth of the national average. This paucity of people may not always please the chamber of commerce, but for those who appreciate human richness as well as natural splendor while on a trip away from home, the Mountain North is guaranteed to please.

"The Mountain North," Neil Morgan once wrote, "still belongs to God. Its population is thin, and when one does not see a human being for a good many miles, the human seems more important. Values count more than they do in places where people begin to get in each other's way—and that will not change in the Mountain North, not for a long time."

If you're vacationing in these states, plan to spend a lot of time on the highway. There's a lot of space between cities. On a TV documentary about Montana, to prove the point, a young schoolteacher complained that her largest monthly expense was her telephone bill. She frequently called a close friend, another teacher, who was her nearest neighbor. The "neighbor," she explained, lived 50 miles away.

The Rockies are one of America's most important landforms. They influence weather systems as they move from one coast to the other, sometimes dramatically changing from one side of a mountain slope to the other. In historic times, the Rockies were a major obstacle to westward migration. Were it not for the stubborn persistence of explorers like Meriwether Lewis and William Clark, the Mountain North may well have been left in the custody of its Indians for another half century or more. Even today, the vertical geography of the Rocky Mountain states is a discouragement to settlement in many places.

The Mountain North represents roughly the upper third of an eight-state mountain empire—those states touched or influenced by the Rockies—which in turn occupies nearly 30 percent of all states that lie between the Atlantic and Pacific oceans.

Along the rim of the Rockies is the Continental Divide, an invisible line that in the contiguous states extends from the Animas Mountains of southwestern New Mexico to the Lewis Range in Montana. The Continental Divide follows the ridge of this great mountain chain (but not always at the highest peaks) and separates the rivers that flow on one side into the Pacific Ocean and Gulf of California and those flowing on the other into the Gulf of Mexico. The highest points of the Divide are in Colorado, where every one of the Rockies exceeding 14,000 feet in elevation is found. The Rockies descend gradually in elevation as they march north toward Canada, though height is not necessarily a valid yardstick for measuring a mountain's splendor or ruggedness, as any first-time visitor to Grand Teton and Yellowstone National Parks in Wyoming will agree.

In the Mountain North, the Continental Divide separates the watersheds of two major river systems. One is the Upper Columbia Basin whose waters, gathered from many smaller streams, drain into the Pacific at the common border between Oregon and Washington—the Columbia River. The other, the Upper Missouri Basin, collects all the runoff from an even broader region. The tributary streams feed into the Missouri at some point, travel 2,700 miles to the Missouri's confluence with the Mississippi River near St. Louis, then drain another 1,200 miles to the Gulf of Mexico. That's 3,900 miles altogether. In the 19th Century, Henry Schoolcraft followed the Mississippi River northward and declared its origin to be at Lake Itasca in Minnesota. But there are some geographers who argue that Schoolcraft followed the lesser of the two rivers and that he should have traced the Missouri to its headwaters in Wyoming instead. Had that happened, the visitor who stands today on the eastern slope of the Continental Divide in Wyoming could be viewing the genesis trickle of the world's longest river.

No matter. The Mountain North has enough going for it without fretting over the loss of just one of its many possible superlatives.

It encompasses, for instance, three of the nation's greatest national parks: Yellowstone, in Wyoming, is not only the largest of all national parks south of Alaska, it was also the first national park in the world; Glacier, joined with Canada's Waterton Lakes National Park, is the world's first peace park; and there is also Grand Teton, home of the national elk herd, whose jagged peaks seem clawed by a giant hand.

The Mountain North is rich in mineral wealth; it is no mere coincidence that Montana is known as the Treasure State, and Idaho, as the Gem State. And forests. Nearly 55 million acres in these three states are tree-covered contrasting with vast stretches of desert plateau.

Altogether, the Mountain North extends about 650 miles wide from the golden prairies of eastern Montana and Wyoming to Idaho's Hell's Canyon and the Snake River that winds through it. It's the deepest gorge in America, in fact, deeper (though not wider) than Arizona's Grand Canyon, and there are parts of the wilderness nearby that can be reached only by pack animal or on foot.

But more than any other single feature, it is the Rockies themselves which dominate the landscape of the Mountain North. How they came to be is a story that dates back about one billion years. Depending upon the specific region, it involved various mountain-building processes: uplifting, faulting, folding, volcanism and glaciation.

The heaviest concentration of volcanic activity was in what is today southern Idaho, extending northeasterly to present-day Yellowstone National Park. Today's traveler need not worry that he'll be scorched by a volcano, but he can see living proof of this fiery period in earth's history in the geysers and hot springs of Yellowstone.

Evidence of faulting and folding is visible throughout the Mountain North. Sometimes the process left a smooth,

54

clean surface. In other places, like the Tetons, slopes and peaks were twisted into wild, uneven shapes that became a mountain climber's Holy Grail.

The final stage of glaciation occurred during the Ice Ages, the last of which ended 12,000 to 15,000 years ago. Working more ponderously than volcanism, glaciers—huge blocks of water frozen during a dramatic global climate change—"fine-tuned" the mountain landscape: carving rock, smoothing the bottoms of V-shaped canyons into U-shaped ones, leaving huge piles of debris called moraines in their wake.

Weather and climate in the Mountain North vary widely depending upon both location and altitude. Weather can be very severe, especially in winter.

Mountain North climate as well as that throughout the Rockies is generally drier than that in the Pacific Coast states since much of the moisture in clouds carried eastward has already been wrung out by the Cascades and other mountain ranges farther west.

Part of the Mountain North is semi-desert. The Big Horn and Great Divide Basins of Wyoming, as an example, are among the driest regions of the entire Rockies. Yet when storms do occur, they can be violent. Egg-sized hailstones in Idaho have become almost as famous as that state's potatoes.

For the outdoorsman, there's a lot to see and do in the Mountain North and although highway distances are sometimes long, the state and federal highway system is such that loop-trip planning may include many destinations on the same vacation.

In addition to the three national parks, much of the land in the Mountain North is devoted to national forests and state parks, and historic sites abound, especially those which preserve the legacy of cowboys, Indians and explorers. The needs of skiers aren't overlooked either; Schweitzer Basin in northern Idaho and the Big Mountain area south of Glacier National Park in Montana are increasingly popular winter sports spas, and Sun Valley, also in Idaho, has been famous since the Thirties.

Counting the national parks, there are 14 sites in the three states of the Mountain North administered by the National Park Service. Eliminating the parks—all of them heavily visited and crowded in summer—leaves 11 sites. Significantly, all but 2 of them are listed by the NPS in its booklet, "The National Parks: Lesser-Known Areas." One criterion for including sites in this interesting publication is visitation—or, more accurately, the lack of it. To the traveler who shuns crowds that should send a message loud and clear: except for the three national parks, where off-season visiting may be preferred, here is a vast region of the country whose historic, recreational and geologic sites seem to be begging for visitors. Yet many of these are on or near highway routes which the motorist must follow to reach Yellowstone, Glacier or Grand Teton National Parks.

Here are just a few samples of lesser-known areas where you can go almost any time of year without rubbing elbows with other visitors.

Three of the sites—one in Idaho, two in Montana—relate to the history and culture of Western Indians and their relationship with the white man. Nez Perce National Historic Park in the northwestern "panhandle" of Idaho preserves the history of the Nez Perce tribes.

In southwestern Montana, Big Hole National Battlefield, established in 1910, marks the area where the Nez Perce ended their long struggle against white domination. A 22½-mile trail follows the route of the Nez Perce's last war. Perhaps the most famous Indian battle of all is memorialized at Custer Battlefield National Monument, in the southeast section of Montana. It was here on June 25–26, 1876, that U.S. Army Lt. Col. George A. Custer and about 268 of his troops were killed by Indians in the famous Battle of the Little Big Horn.

Craters of the Moon National Monument, near Arco, Idaho, is a landscape of volcanic cones, lava flows and caves—evidence of early volcanism. More traces of volcanic activity can be seen in northeast Wyoming at Devils Tower National Monument. Here is an 865-foot-high column of rock that is all that remains of a major, long-ago volcanic intrusion. If you are keen on geology, consider a stopover at Fossil Butte National Monument in southwestern Wyoming, while en route to or returning from Grand Teton or Yellowstone National Parks. Here is the country's most extensive concentration of fossilized freshwater fish, imbedded in shale 60 million years old.

Finally, there is Bighorn Canyon National Recreation Area in southern Montana, near that state's border with Wyoming. Including a 47-mile section through spectacular Bighorn Canyon, the NRA is 71 miles long altogether, formed by the Yellowtail Dam on the Bighorn River. Boating, camping, picnicking, fishing, hunting and boat rentals are available here. Bighorn Canyon is the only national recreation area in the three-state Mountain North of the unhurried American West.

55

Glacier National Park

True wilderness knows no political boundaries, whether between states or between nations. Two national parks on the U.S.-Canadian border—Glacier in the United States and Waterton Lakes in Canada—are an excellent case in point. The mighty Rocky Mountains heed no customs rules in their march north to south from British Columbia to Montana, nor do the bald eagles, elk and trout that fly, walk or swim across the 49th Parallel, which since 1818 has formed the boundary between them.

Merged in a common union of uncommon mountains, glacier-sculptured valleys, lush conifer forests, prairie grasslands, primitive trails and icy lakes and streams, these two national parks offer some of the most scenic wilderness in either country, though on a map they are separated by an international border. Since 1932, however, Glacier and Waterton Lakes have had even more in common than their natural heritage. Symbolizing both the spirit of friendship between the United States and Canada and the wilderness ethic of their peoples, they are designated jointly as the Waterton/Glacier International Peace Park, the first such park in the world.

The parks are administered separately by the United States and Canada, though by both international agreement and working policy, visitors may cross from one park to the other with little formality. On an excursion boat plying Upper Waterton Lake, about half its length in each country, there are no formalities at all; on a hiking trail which parallels the lake's west shore, hikers may "clear" into their neighboring country before leaving their own. Such is the ease with which visitors may experience the awe-some grandeur of these parks which have so much in common.

Partly because of its location, away from major transcontinental highway routes, Glacier draws fewer than 1.6 million visitors a year, compared to 2.4 million at better-known Yellowstone and 3 million at Yosemite National Park. Glacier, therefore, is not as crowded as some other parks, considering size for size, but visitors who dislike crowds can reduce the odds of elbow-rubbing even further by scheduling an off-season visit.

Glacier's peak season occurs in July and August. The lowest, in terms of people, is from January to March. Not only are crowds smaller in winter, late fall and spring, but there are other advantages. Wildlife photography is better, for instance, and the hiker or skier will find a measure of peace and beauty here not always possible in midsummer.

The park does experience severe weather, however, sometimes even in summer. Visitors should be prepared for it. Temperatures can plummet dramatically when an Arctic-born weather front bustles through, with rain accompanied by lightning, snow and sleet. Most park roads are closed from late fall to early June, as are most facilities except for two campgrounds. That still leaves plenty of visiting time between the end of the busy summer season and the first snow, and a short "time window" between the end of spring and the arrival of the first summer visitors after schools close. For the skier, snowshoer or off-season hiker and backpacker, of course, winter is the best time, assuming he has prepared himself for Glacier's often severe weather.

Like most national parks, Glacier is a place whose beauty can be savored either by vehicle or on foot.

In season, when it is open, the splendid Going-to-the-Sun Road offers some of the finest scenery in any national park, and the story of its construction in the Twenties and Thirties is a book in itself. From the park's western entrance at West Glacier, Going-to-the-Sun traverses 51 miles of the park at St. Mary on the eastern boundary, climbing to an elevation of 6,680 feet at Logan Pass where there is a visitor center.

Civilian Conservation Corps crews blasted the route of Going-to-the-Sun against enormous odds, running up a construction bill of $3 million before the road was finished. In Logan Pass they had to dynamite their way through limestone rock, often working in terrible weather. Today's visitors may travel a part of the road in Thirties-style convertible buses known as "Reds" (because of their color) whose drivers are still referred to as "jammers." In the off-season, however, Going-to-the-Sun is kept open only from West Glacier to Lake McDonald Lodge—about 10 miles.

Hikers have more than 700 miles of maintained trails to choose from in Glacier and Waterton National Parks. Those at lower elevations are usually passable by mid-June, though snow may linger in high-country passes until late July.

There are many styles of camping available in Glacier, too, from those offering full conveniences to primitive backpacking. Eight campgrounds can be reached by paved road; those with fewer amenities, via gravel road or on foot.

There are eight lodges in the two national parks, each with a distinct architectural motif and interior decor. Four of them date back almost to the opening of Glacier National Park in 1910, and all are worth visiting, even if not staying over-

Pat O'Hara

ST. MARY LAKE *from Goose Island Overlook in Glacier National Park. The lake generally parallels the eastern portion of Going-to-the-Sun Highway starting at the St. Mary Visitor Center entrance to the Montana park.*

night. The impetus for lodge building was that of the Great Northern Railway, whose route ran along the southern edge of Glacier, which hoped to attract railway revenue as well as to call attention to Glacier as a well-deserved outdoor wonder of America. Glacier Park Lodge, at the park's eastern entrance, is situated at the edge of the Blackfoot Indian Reservation and has an American Indian motif. In 1915, Many Glacier Hotel was opened on Swiftcurrent Lake; decorative Swiss emblems remind guests how much the area resembles the Alps of Europe. Lake McDonald Lodge, begun as a fishing camp in 1913, has many animal heads and fishing trophies on its lobby walls. On the Canadian side, the Great Northern Railway built the magnificent Prince of Wales Hotel, opened in 1928, four years before the parks were joined as a friendship symbol of the two countries.

Because of the wide range of climates and altitudes, flora and fauna in the two parks are very diverse. On western mountain slopes, for instance, will be found dense forests of spruce, fir and lodgepole pine. Species which require less moisture grow on the opporite side. Alpine areas stimulate some of the best wildflower growth in North America: heather, gentian, beargrass and glacier lily. In eastern meadows, where the plains roll up to join the mountains, such prairie flowers as pasqueflowers, geraniums, asters, shooting stars and Indian paintbrush can be found.

Both grizzly and black bear live in the parks. Needless to say, they are wild animals and must not be approached. Feeding any animal is against park regulations. Other wildlife includes bighorn sheep, mountain goat, elk, moose and deer. Beaver, marmot, river otter, mar-

ten and pika are numbered among the parks' smaller mammals. Visitors on the Canadian side may see a small herd of buffalo in a paddock near the Townsite.

Fish species include pike, whitefish and several varieties of trout—rainbow, eastern brook, and cutthroat. The most popular fishing areas are Cameron Lake, Waterton River and the lakes of Waterton Valley.

Boating is a popular summer activity, with rental canoes and rowboats available at most of the larger U.S. lakes and (in Canada), "ponds." Motorboats and waterskiing are allowed only on the Upper and Middle Waterton Lakes. The two parks have plenty of water area for swimming, but most visitors wouldn't want to try it; since most lakes and rivers are glacier-fed, it's much too chilly.

Winter visitors gain an entirely different perspective of the parks than those who arrive in summer. Cross-country skiing and snowshoeing are popular; both parks have some programs going even after most facilities are closed.

Glacier National Park West Glacier, MT 59936, (406) 888-5441

Access: In the U.S., reached from U.S. Hwy. 2 and 89; in Canada, from Alta. 5, 6 and 3.

Season: Park open all year. Most roads closed in winter, except one between the park headquarters and Lake McDonald Lodge. Severe storms even in summer, with low temperatures, rain, snow, sleet and lightning.

Visitor Centers: St. Mary, late May to mid-October; Logan Pass, mid-June to mid-September. Information center open late May through mid-December at Apgar, open Saturdays and Sundays only during winter.

Lodging: St. Mary, Glacier, East Glacier. Concessioner accommodations include hotels, lodges, chalets and cabins. Reservations advised; write (May 15 to Sept. 15) Glacier Park, Inc., East Glacier Park, MT 59434; or (Sept. 15 to May 15) Greyhound Tower, Station 5510, Phoenix, AZ 85077. Sperry and Granite Park Chalets open for backcountry travelers July 1 through Labor Day, accessible by trail only. For rates and reservations, contact Belton Chalets, P.O. Box 188, West Glacier, MT 59936. For Waterton accommodations, write the Waterton Chamber of Commerce, Waterton Park, Alberta TOK 2MO.

Camping: 1,127 sites or spaces throughout park, including backcountry camps. Sites at Apgar, St. Mary Lake open only according to season. No reservations.

Services: Meals at Apgar, Swiftcurrent, Rising Sun, Many Glacier, Lake McDonald. Food and supplies at Rising Sun, Apgar, Swiftcurrent and Two Medicine. Food and supplies nearby: West Glacier, East Glacier, St. Mary.

Activities: Biking, horseback riding and tours, excursion boat cruises, fishing, cross-country skiing, snowshoeing, camping, hiking (700 miles of maintained trails) and interpretive exhibits.

For further information on permits, fees, reservations, winter activities and park regulations, write or call park headquarters.

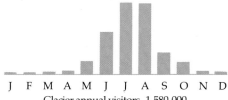

J F M A M J J A S O N D
Glacier annual visitors, 1,580,000

Pat O'Hara

FALL COLORS *of trees on hillsides near Avalanche Lake (left) are an enticement for an off-season visit. At the right, Lunch Creek tumbles over a series of rock terraces. Scalloped ridges of Little Chief Mountain are captured in half-sunlight, half-shadow (below).*

Pat O'Hara

Pat O'Hara

Yellowstone National Park

Artists have preserved it on canvas, poets in words, photographers on film. For more than a century since its founding in 1872, writers have struggled to define its almost magical appeal to the human spirit, scientists, to plumb its geological mysteries. Yet Yellowstone National Park—birthplace of a dream and a conservation ethic that has since taken root and blossomed worldwide—must be seen to be believed.

It is not Yellowstone's size alone that awes, overwhelms and inspires, though any park larger than Rhode Island and Delaware combined must humble the visitor by sheer geographic audacity. Nor is it only its mountains, conifer forests, waterfalls, rivers, meadows and glacial canyons, any one of which another park might covet. Nor the fire and brimstone origins which account for the 10,000 thermal features for which Yellowstone is perhaps best known. Nor its varied inventory of wildlife, or any of the other superlatives, such as the fossil forests which cover more than 40 square miles of park land, the largest of its kind known anywhere on earth.

Any one of these features by itself would make Yellowstone National Park unique in the truest sense of that overused word. Combined, they serve to mark it as one of the world's great natural treasures.

Yellowstone is the largest national park in the lower 48 states, and the first established in the world. It covers 3,472 square miles in all, about midway along the northern Rocky Mountains. It sprawls squarely across the Continental Divide. In elevation, the park ranges from about 5,000 feet, near North Entrance, to the summit of 11,358-foot Eagle Peak near the southern boundary; the average elevation is about 7,500 feet. Early Indians called this region the "summit of the world."

Snow has been recorded in every month of the year, and raging blizzards can occur even in June and July. The heaviest annual snowfall on record was more than 22 feet, recorded at the Lake Ranger Station in 1922; doubtless, snowfall heavier than 30 feet has occurred at higher elevations.

The annual Yellowstone precipitation varies between 14 and 38 inches, accounting for tremendous spring runoffs which have encouraged a great assemblage of plant and animal life.

Yellowstone is simply too large, too varied, too complex to be visited hurriedly. To gain an overall perspective in a short time, auto touring is a must, although Yellowstone's snow season—December through April—limits the car-bound visitor somewhat. However, for the off-season visitor there is much to see along the one park road maintained throughout the year, that from North Entrance at Gardiner to Cooke City, Montana, just outside Northeast Entrance. It runs through Mammoth Hot Springs, where park headquarters are located.

This is not to suggest that Yellowstone shuts down in winter. Definitely, it does not. Cross-country skiing, snowshoeing and snowmobiling are popular winter activities and, even viewed from a distance, the plateau and mountain country of Yellowstone beneath a mantle of winter white is breathtaking.

Fortunately, due both to its size and heavy visitation (about 2.4 million people a year), Yellowstone has been able to justify a road system ideally suited for sampling the major features via car, as well as one of the most extensive interpretation programs of any national park. There are five visitor centers at widely separated locations, plus two special interest museums. All are located on the loop road which encircles the park's midsection. All make available the usual visitor aids such as leaflets, publications, maps and exhibits, but each in addition has a special display interpreting a particular phase of Yellowstone National Park, for the benefit of the visitor with a special interest, and all are open year-round.

Grand Loop Road circles 142 miles around the middle of Yellowstone National Park. It connects with access roads leading in from all five park entrances. In addition, there is a 12-mile road from Norris to Canyon Village which links the eastern and western lengths of the loop, turning it into a Figure-8. Grand Loop can be driven in a long, leisurely day, and there are many pull-outs from which major features of the park—mountains, the Grand Canyon of the Yellowstone, plateaus, lakes, thermal hot spots—can be seen. However, only a 56-mile section of the loop, from the North Entrance to Tower-Roosevelt, and east to Cooke City, Montana is open to cars during the snow season.

Loop Road can be divided into three sections. The first extends 90 miles along the west side of the park from South Entrance to Mammoth Hot Springs, via Old Faithful and Madison. South Entrance is less than 10 miles from Grand Teton National Park. Most visitors combine a visit to the two parks (encouraging this habit, the National Park Service charges only one entrance fee for both parks, valid seven days).

The loop section includes five geyser

basins—West Thumb, Upper (Old Faithful), Midway, Lower and Norris—before Mammoth. Geysers, of which Old Faithful is the best known, are a special and relatively rare kind of thermal hot spring, spewing water and steam as high as 180 feet in the air. There are geysers in the world more faithful than Old Faithful (in terms of the predictability of their geysering), but none more famous. Old Faithful's eruption intervals have long varied around an average of 65 minutes. Earthquakes in 1959 and 1983 upset the schedules of many Yellowstone geysers; Old Faithful now spouts about every 72 minutes, spring, summer, fall and winter, but off-season is best to avoid crowds.

From Madison to Norris, the Loop Road passes along the northwest rim of Yellowstone's giant caldera (volcanic basin). The caldera—30 by 40 miles in size—resulted from the last, most gigantic of a series of volcanic eruptions which shaped the landscape here more than any other geologic force. Volcanic blasts, some so violent they hurtled about 240 cubic miles of debris as far as the Mississippi Delta, occurred first about 2 million years ago, then 1.2 million years ago, and, finally, about 600,000 years ago.

At Norris, you can turn east across the road connecting the Figure-8, with its east end at Canyon, or continue another 21 miles north to Mammoth. If choosing the latter, you'll pass Obsidian Cliff, named for a volcanic glass which Indians used for spear points and cutting tools, and, via a one-way detour, another thermal area where limber pines have been growing for 500 years. At Mammoth, the end of the first loop section, are spectacular terraces of travertine, a calcium carbonate, to which present thermal activity

Fred Hirschmann

61

THE SEASONS *may come and go in Yellowstone National Park, and so may the visitors, but Old Faithful remains true to its name, whatever the weather and whatever the time of year. This photograph was taken on a subzero winter afternoon.*

is adding new surface every day.

The second section of the loop extends 18 miles east from Mammoth to Tower, then another 19 miles south from Tower to Canyon Village, the heart of Yellowstone's wildlife country. Just east of Mammoth, you may spot muskrats and waterfowl at Blacktail Ponds; bison, mule deer and elk are also common along this route, and occasionally antelope and bighorn sheep. These are most easily seen in spring among the wildflowers and in fall beneath the quaking

aspen shimmering in their coats of gold.

South of Tower, Antelope and Tower Creeks are in the heart of grizzly bear country. The area on either side of the road is closed to humans for an obvious reason: grizzlies are dangerous.

Canyon lies at the southern end of the Grand Canyon of the Yellowstone, a spectacular chasm 20 miles long and more than 1,000 feet deep. Its vivid colors were created by hot water working against volcanic rock. There are two superb lookout points at Canyon where

Fred Hirschmann

62   WILDLIFE AND WATER, *the two most striking themes of Yellowstone National Park to many visitors, are dramatically illustrated in these five photographs. Clockwise from top left: in late afternoon, storm clouds gather along Soda Butte Creek while a waning sun casts its glow against a solitary tree; Lower Falls of the Yellowstone River as seen from Artist Point; Flat Mountain Arm of Yellowstone Lake is tranquil and serene in early*

Pat O'Hara

Fred Hirschmann

Fred Hirschmann

morning; a cow elk is silhouetted by sun rays streaming through a morning fog; for the fisherman, Yellowstone's waters mean only one thing: a chance to bag one of the park's three species of cutthroat trout (named for the red marks on their lower jaws) which, along with the mountain whitefish, are all native to Yellowstone. Moose, bison, grizzly bear and bighorn sheep are other animals for which Yellowstone has long been noted. A land use model for many nations, this national park—first in the United States—is both an important wildlife refuge and an International Biosphere Reserve.

63

Fred Hirschmann

the canyon and waterfalls may be seen.

Hayden Valley, south of Canyon, follows the Yellowstone River along a glaciated former lakebed, then on upstream to Yellowstone Lake, largest mountain lake in the United States. Smaller now than in ancient times, the lake still measures an impressive 20 by 14 miles. Boating is permitted, as is fishing (Yellowstone has, for instance, three native subspecies of cutthroat trout), although there are boat restrictions in the southern portion of the lake. In season, boat tours are popular on Yellowstone.

White pelicans, Canadian geese and other waterfowl abound in marshy areas along the lakefront; moose, bison and occasional grizzly bears may also be seen.

The last section of the loop trip takes the visitor along the west side of Yellowstone Lake to Grant Village. This segment can be reached via East Entrance, 53 miles from Cody, Wyoming. If you arrive from the east, you'll drive over 8,530-foot-high Sylvan Pass where, on the rocky debris of talus slopes, you may spot pikas and marmots, among the smallest of Yellowstone's mammals.

As extensive as it is, Loop Road affords the visitor just one dimension of spectacular Yellowstone National Park. The park itself supports perhaps more visitor amenities—lodges, gas stations, restaurants, churches, even auto repair garages—than do most national parks, and some are open even in winter.

For visitors who shun this kind of pampering, however, much of Yellowstone represents the same kind of wilderness that fascinated its first white explorers in the 19th Century. There are 1,000 miles of hiking trails here, hundreds of square miles of primitive backcountry most visitors never see. Lit-

tle wonder that even after a century as a national park, Yellowstone remains, in the words of England's Prince Philip, a devoted admirer, "an inspiration and confirmation that dreams are made to come true."

Yellowstone National Park P.O. Box 168, Yellowstone National Park, WY 82190, (307) 344-7381

Access: By auto: from the north by U.S. 89; from the northeast by U.S. 212; from the east through Cody, U.S. 20, 14 and 16 merged; from the south via the John D. Rockefeller Jr. Memorial Parkway, U.S. 89 and U.S. 287 and U.S. 191; and from the west via West Yellowstone, U.S. 191 and 20. By air: flights to nearby Billings, Bozeman and West Yellowstone, Montana; to Cody and Jackson Hole, Wyoming.

Season: Portions of park open all year. Roads open to auto traffic are Gardiner to Mammoth and on to the Northeast Entrance and Cooke City, Montana. Other park entrances and roads for autos closed by snow from Oct. 31 to May 1 (approximate). In winter, visitors may enter the park by heated oversnow coaches from West Yellowstone, Mammoth Hot Springs and South Entrance.

Visitor Centers: At Mammoth Hot Springs, Old Faithful, Canyon, Grant Village and Fishing Bridge. Museums at Mammoth, Madison Junction, Norris.

Lodging: In park: hotels, lodges, cabins and a trailer park, open mid-June through Labor Day. Lodging is available through the winter at Old Faithful and Mammoth Hot Springs Hotel. Reservations are advised. Write: TW Services, Inc., Yellowstone National Park, WY 82190, phone (307) 344-7311. Nearby: Gardiner, Cooke City/Silvergate, Liv-

ingston, Bozeman, West Yellowstone and Red Lodge in Montana; Cody and Jackson in Wyoming.

Camping: Many campgrounds throughout the park, Mammoth campground (½ mile N of Mammoth Junction) is open year-round. Bridge Bay (3 miles SW of Lake Village), Madison (¼ mile W of Madison Junction) and Slough Creek (10 miles NE of Tower Fall Junction) are open from about May to October. Nine other facilities open June–September.

Services: In park: meals served at Lake, Canyon, Tower-Roosevelt, Mammoth Hot Springs, Old Faithful and Grant Village. Food and supplies at Lake, Fishing Bridge, Canyon, Tower-Roosevelt, Tower Falls, West Thumb, Mammoth Hot Springs, Grant Village and Old Faithful. Nearby: Livingston, Bozeman, Gardiner, West Yellowstone, Red Lodge and Cooke City/Silvergate, Montana; Cody and Jackson in Wyoming.

Activities: Driving, hiking, horseback-riding, bird and wildlife watching, fishing, boating, biking, stagecoach rides, snowmobiling, skiing, snowshoeing, winter walks, backpacking. Many boat and bus tours, interpretive and campfire programs, and learning seminars are available.

For further information on permits, fees, camping and park regulations, write or call park headquarters.

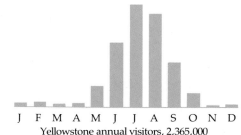

Yellowstone annual visitors, 2,365,000

64

WILDLIFE'S GOLDEN CIRCLE.

Place the point of a draftsman's compass in the center of a map of Yellowstone National Park, about where Fishing Bridge is located, and draw a circle with a radius representing 50 miles. On the northern part of the circle you'll include the Beartooth, Gallatin and Madison mountain ranges, outside the park in Montana; on the southern, Grand Teton National Park and the Teton and Wind River Ranges of Wyoming. The circle will also include parts of at least four national forests which surround Yellowstone.

What you have just drawn encompasses, in a very approximate way, an area biologists call the Greater Yellowstone Ecosystem. In terms of wild creatures that have survived 20th Century human encroachment, it is one of the last, few remaining, great wilderness areas in the Lower 48 States.

You'll find wildlife in many Western national parks. Nowhere, however, will it be found in as great a profusion as in this magic circle of the American wild: grizzly and black bear, moose, elk, deer, American bison, bighorn sheep, waterfowl, bald eagles, trumpeter swans and pronghorn antelope, to name a few. Yellowstone is one of only two areas of the contiguous states that support grizzly populations (the other is Glacier National Park in Montana). It is one of the last natural refuges of the American buffalo, or bison, a Great Plains animal whose number once exceeded 60 million, reduced to a mere 300 by 1900. The trumpeter swan, one of Yellowstone's most graceful birds, was as endangered in the United States. Plumage hunters reduced its number to less than 100 individuals until the creation of a National Wildlife Refuge at Red Rocks Lakes helped it make a comeback.

In many ways, then, the Greater Yellowstone Ecosystem, because of the area's relative isolation, its protective perimeter of high mountains, its elevation and its harsh climate, has indeed become one of the most important sanctuaries for wild creatures in North America.

Fred Hirschmann

Fred Hirschmann

Fred Hirschmann

If you prefer to hunt with camera instead of rifle, you're welcome to stalk all the game you want in this perfect circle of wildlife, remembering, of course, that some animals like the grizzly can be wild and dangerous. Which animals you'll see depends on where you are, the time of year, even the time of day. Yellowstone rangers advise that early morning and late afternoon usually are best, and that the wildlife parade is best in summer and fall, the latter being the time when migratory species begin moving toward their wintering grounds.

Rangers will also advise you of the best places to find desired species. But don't limit your "hunt" to the park alone; many animals such as the grizzly need a much wider range and will be found outside Yellowstone as well.

On any given summer or fall day in the Yellowstone area, you may see moose feeding or bison roaming in Hayden Valley, waterfowl along the Yellowstone River, coyotes in Lamar Valley, pronghorn antelope on the sagebrush flats near the North Entrance, bighorn sheep grazing on the slopes of Mount Washburn, bald eagles soaring overhead. Elk and, occasionally, bison may be seen in the Lewis River environs near the South Entrance. And in winter, the wapiti herd gathered on the National Elk Refuge in Jackson Hole, near Grand Teton National Park, is a sight not to be missed.

WILDLIFE ABOUNDS in Yellowstone National Park and the wilderness nearby, making this region one of the greatest natural "zoos" in North America. From top to bottom here are three examples: two bull moose feed in the Yellowstone River in Hayden Valley; bighorn rams lock horns near Gardiner, Montana; an old bison on a frosty morning, also in Hayden Valley. Bison once roamed the American Plains 60 million strong before hunting decimated their number to only 300 or so individuals.

65

Grand Teton National Park

Grand Teton National Park in north-western Wyoming, a roughly rectangular landscape 485 square miles in area, superbly combines some of the best of Western outdoor grandeur: a range of blue-grey, perennially snow-clad mountains, the sagebrush-covered floor of Jackson Hole, several tumbling rivers and placid alpine lakes, America's largest herd of elk, and an abundance of other wildlife large and small.

Especially in summer, Grand Teton is a very popular national park. About two million people visit here annually. Most of them—an estimated 80 percent—combine their vacation with a visit to the larger, older, perhaps better known Yellowstone National Park, a 7½-mile auto drive to the north via the John D. Rockefeller Jr. Memorial Parkway. But although the parks share much in common, they are not the same. Each has many distinct features and the vacationer who doesn't visit both parks in the same trip is missing one of the best bets in the National Park System.

Although Congress designated a mountain area of the Grand Tetons as a national park in 1929, it was not until 1950 that the valley floor—Jackson Hole, a former fur-trading center and a legend of the wild and woolly West—was drawn within its boundaries. That Jackson Hole was added at all, in the face of many developmental pressures (Jackson Lake, for instance, was dammed as early as 1916), was due primarily to the efforts of philanthropist/businessman John D. Rockefeller Jr. who was taken by the region's beauty and park potential during a visit in 1926. Rockefeller began buying up parcels of land in Jackson Hole, offering to deed them to the federal government to add to the then-existing park. Rockefeller's gift—32,189 acres—was finally accepted in 1949 and formally added to the park a year later.

The main land area of the 82-mile-long parkway bearing his name—24,000 acres generally along the Snake River—was designated as a National Park Service site in 1972. Altogether, the federal government had been involved in land management in the region since the 19th Century, when it became apparent that exploitation could damage the critical Snake River watershed. Today, Grand Teton National Park is almost surrounded by national forest; in addition, the 25,000-acre National Elk Refuge, winter home to 7,500 migratory elk, is managed by the U.S. Fish and Wildlife Service outside the park in the southeast corner of Jackson Hole.

Some national parks excel for their wilderness value. In others, recreation is the major attraction. Grand Teton offers both: camping, backpacking, hiking, boating, snow sports, wildlife and bird watching, fishing, mountaineering . . . and incomparable vistas to photograph or preserve on the artist's canvas.

Because of its isolated location and its elevation (from 6,500 feet in Jackson Hole to 13,770 feet at the summit of Grand Teton), weather and season are definite limiting factors to a visit here. The administering National Park Service in fact does not promote winter visitation. Like many national parks, its staff is reduced in winter and many of its facilities shut down. Only a few roads are plowed. However, winter sports, including cross-country skiing, are enjoying increasing popularity; just outside the park, in the community of Jackson, downhill skiing attracts thousands in winter. Grand Teton is one of the few national parks which allows snowmobiling. The activity is limited to unplowed roads, and a permit is required. Sleigh touring is also popular.

Weather can be severe indeed in the Tetons. There are, in fact, few places as cold as Jackson Hole in midwinter, and even in summer sudden thundershowers are common. Sometimes, snow falls as late as May and June. Because the summer season *is* often short, most of the annual visitation is compressed into the space of a couple of months. Facilities are crowded; some park campgrounds are filled by noon, and the more popular trails are clogged.

Midwinter weather discourages many. Seldom does the temperature rise above freezing and subzero readings are common. Blizzards can last for days.

Yet it was this very kind of weather, even colder, in fact, to which the Tetons owe much of their magnificent beauty and visitor appeal. Jackson Hole has undergone three periods of glaciation, the last occurring 65,000 to 12,000 years ago. As the snowpack became heavier, glacial ice formed. Pulled down by gravity, Ice Age glaciers inched slowly down the mountains, carving the skyscraping peaks and the broad, U-shaped canyons such as Granite, Cascade and Moran. Later, as the glaciers melted, they filled depressions in the valley which became today's lakes such as Phelps, Taggart, Bradley, Jenny, Leigh and, largest of them all, Jackson.

You'll see only small remnants of the glaciers in a visit to Grand Teton today. Two of them, Teton and Falling Ice Glaciers, are remnants of the mini-Ice Age which occurred only about 2,000 years ago (in geologic terms, that's a very short

Pat O'Hara

FLOWING FROM *north to south to eventually empty into the Columbia River, the Snake River is the major river in Grand Teton National Park. Its headwaters are formed in Yellowstone National Park.*

time indeed). Could all this happen again? Some scientists say that it could; an annual temperature drop of only 2–3 degrees could again bury this great landscape under a blanket of ice.

But that's not likely to happen for a long, long time. Meanwhile, there are two seasons—spring and fall—which nature seems to have expertly tailored just for the visitor who wants to avoid summer's crowds.

The arrival of spring in Jackson Hole is heralded by the bloom of buttercups and purple shooting stars. At higher elevations, a little later, can be found alpine forget-me-nots, blue columbine and glacier lily (summer flowers in the park include blue lupine, larkspur, wild buckwheat and Wyoming's state flower, the Indian paintbrush).

In spring, animals that hibernate through the winter—the marmot and ground squirrel are two—emerge to forage on early wildflowers. And, as the season begins to move even closer to summer, Grand Teton's elk begin migrating to higher ground from their winter refuge at Jackson Hole.

To many visitors, however, fall is the best time of all to schedule a visit to the Tetons. Autumn colors are spectacular both in Jackson Hole and in the mountains; Oxbow Bend and along the Snake River and Cottonwood Creek are favorite places to see nature's great botanical show. Now the elk herd reverses its spring pattern, moving down from the summer highlands to winter quarters in the refuge. The elk migration is at its peak in November. In winter, touring the refuge in an old-fashioned sleigh is one of the region's special activities. Large, social animals whose males weigh between 550 and 1,000 pounds, the elk

68

Pat O'Hara

BALSAMROOT *wildflowers (left) mark the Grand Teton spring with a splash of golden color. At right, snowshoes and cross-country skis replace hiking shoes for backcountry winter exploring. Far right, the snow-clad peaks of the Tetons bask in sunlight. The Cathedral group of the Tetons as viewed from Schwabacher Landing (both pages).*

Pat O'Hara

Pat O'Hara

here form one of the largest herds in North America.

Other large mammals in the park include bighorn sheep (occasionally seen from high country trails), moose, pronghorn antelope, mule deer, bear and mountain lion. About 2,000 bison, remnants of great herds that once roamed the West and Great Plains, are protected in Yellowstone and Grand Teton National Parks. You may also see chipmunks, rabbits, beaver and many other smaller mammals; checklists of mammals and birds (including the bald eagle) are available at visitor centers.

Lodgepole pines are probably the most abundant trees in Jackson Hole; Engelmann spruce, limber and whitebark pines and Douglas fir are also numerous. Willows and quaking aspen line streambanks. The floor of Jackson Hole is covered mainly by sagebrush and bitterbrush.

Grand Teton is a park that invites auto touring. The Rockefeller Parkway extends generally north-south the length of the park. Teton Park Road, with its many scenic pull-outs, runs closer to the base of the mountain range.

But to see Grand Teton's more remote corners, you'll need cross-country skis or good hiking shoes. Hiking is, in fact, the *only* way to see the craggy highlands. There are 200 miles of maintained trail in Grand Teton, covering a wide spectrum of difficulty. An often-recommended "get acquainted" trail is the one which leads from Jenny Lake to Hidden Falls. Requiring about a half-day trip, it gives visitors a capsulized view of the park's three major topographic features: mountains, water and valleys. A shuttleboat ride across Jenny Lake cuts off about four miles of the trip.

69

Pat O'Hara

In summer, floating down the Snake River is popular; commercial float concessioners provide scenic trips. So is canoeing (for the experienced) and boat tours of the park's lakes (no skills required). There are restrictions on boat motors, and only hand-propelled boats are allowed on Emma Matilda, Two Ocean, Bradley, Taggart, Leigh, Bearpaw and String Lakes. Swimming is permitted in the lakes, but even in summer, chilly water temperatures discourage all but the lionhearted. There are no lifeguards.

For those with experience, the Tetons are a superb mountaineer's challenge. Many climbers train here for the Everests and Annapurnas of distant lands. Climbing instruction and guide service is available, and the Tetons seem tailored for just about every degree of scaling skill. A few of the peaks can be climbed in a day, while others require at least an overnight backpacking trip.

Surely, the Teton Range is among the most magnificent mountain ranges on earth. As mountains go, they are not very old, their origin dating back only about nine million years, making them the youngest mountains in the Rocky Mountain chain. Yet by contrast, exposed on their eastern side are some of the oldest rocks in North America, dating back some three billion years.

The Tetons are considered a classic example of fault-block mountain building; that is, they were formed when a huge block of the earth's outer crust fractured, uplifted and tilted the materials which formed the mountains seen today.

Grand Teton National Park P.O. Drawer 170, Moose, WY 83012, (307) 733-2880

Access: From Yellowstone National Park on the north, via the John D. Rockefeller Jr. Memorial Parkway (Rts. 89, 191, 287); from Dubois on the east, via Rts. 26, 287; from Jackson on the south, via Rts. 26, 86, 191).
Season: Park open all year. Many facilities closed Oct. 1–May 15.
Visitor Center: Moose Visitor Center open from 8 A.M. to 4:30 P.M., year-round except Christmas Day. Colter Bay Visitor Center open May 16–Sept. 30.
Lodging: Nearby: Flagg Ranch Village open year round. For reservations, write Flagg Ranch Village, P.O. Box 187, Moran, WY 83013, (800) 443-2311. In park: Jackson Lake Lodge, Jenny Lake Lodge, Colter Bay Cabins and Colter Bay Tent Village, mid-June to mid-Sept. For reservations, write or phone Grand Teton Lodge Co., Box 240, Moran, WY 83013, (307) 543-2855. Signal Mountain Lodge open May 10–Oct. 6. Reservations, write or phone Signal Mountain Lodge, Box 50, Moran, WY 83013, (307) 543-2831.
Camping: There are five campgrounds operated by the National Park Service. Opening dates vary from early May to mid-June. Closing dates from early September to mid-October. Reservations for groups only. A concessioner-operated trailer village with hookups is at Colter Bay. Reservations available by writing the Grand Teton Lodge Co., P.O. Box 240, Moran, WY 83013, (307) 543-2855. More than a dozen U.S. Forest Service and commercial campgrounds are located near the park.
Services: Meals served in the park at Colter Bay and at Jackson Lake, Jenny Lake and Signal Mountain Lodges. Food and supplies obtainable in the park at Colter Bay Village, Jackson Lake, Jenny Lake

and Signal Mountain Lodges; Moose, and Kelley. Nearby at Jackson. Gas available at Colter Bay Village, Jackson Lake Lodge, Signal Mountain Lodge, Flagg Ranch Village, and in Moose and Jackson. All services not available year-round.
Activities: Hiking, backpacking, mountain climbing, horseback riding, boating, river and lake rafting and canoeing trips, fishing, biking, snowmobiling, cross-country skiing (downhill skiing at Jackson), wildlife watching including horse-drawn sleigh rides through the National Elk Refuge (in winter).

For further information on permits, fees, reservations and park regulations, write or call park headquarters.

J F M A M J J A S O N D
Grand Teton annual visitors, 1,310,000

70

Other Selected Sites

IDAHO

Craters of the Moon National Monument P.O. Box 29, Arco, ID 83213. Telephone (208) 527-3257. Eighteen miles west of Arco on U.S. 20, 26 and 93. Spectacular landscape of volcanic cones, craters and caves. Camping and hiking.

Nez Perce National Historical Park P.O. Box 93, Spalding, ID 83551. Telephone (208) 843-2261. Eleven miles east of Lewiston, on U.S. Hwy. 95. Preserves the history and culture of the Nez Perce Indians on 4 federally owned sites and 20 other sites by cooperative agreement, on 12,000 square miles.

MONTANA

Big Hole National Battlefield P.O. Box 237, Wisdom, MT 59761. Telephone (406) 689-3155. Ten miles west of Wisdom. Site of major battle in 1877 between the Nez Perce Indians and the U.S. Army.

Bighorn Canyon National Recreation Area P.O. Box 458, Fort Smith, MT 59035. Telephone (406) 666-2412. Between Hardin and Lowell. Bighorn Lake extends 71 miles behind Yellowtail Dam on the Bighorn River. Year-round water activities, fishing, camping and hiking.

Custer Battlefield National Monument P.O. Box 39, Crow Agency, MT 59022. Telephone (406) 638-2621. On Crow Indian Reservation in southeastern Montana. Site of the famous Battle of Little Bighorn in which Lt. Col. George A. Custer and 268 of his troops were killed.

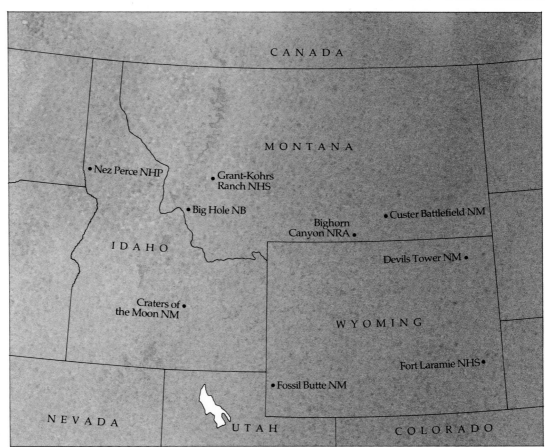

71

Grant-Kohrs Ranch National Historic Site P.O. Box 790, Deer Lodge, MT 59722. Telephone (406) 846-2070. Midway between Glacier and Yellowstone National Parks. In 19th Century, headquarters of a large ranch; the ranch house, bunkhouse and outbuildings have been preserved.

WYOMING

Devils Tower National Monument Devils Tower, WY 82714. Telephone (307) 467-5370. Seven miles north of Sundance. Established in 1906 as the nation's first national monument; its 865-foot-high tower of columnar rock is the remains of a volcanic eruption. Camping and hiking.

Fort Laramie National Historic Site Fort Laramie, WY 82212. Telephone (307) 837-2221. Near Fort Laramie. Preserved buildings of an important military post that protected covered wagon trains in 1849–90. Hiking.

Fossil Butte National Monument P.O. Box 527, Kemmerer, WY 83101. Telephone (307) 877-3450. About 11 miles west of Kemmerer. Rare fish fossils 48–52 million years old are preserved. Hiking.

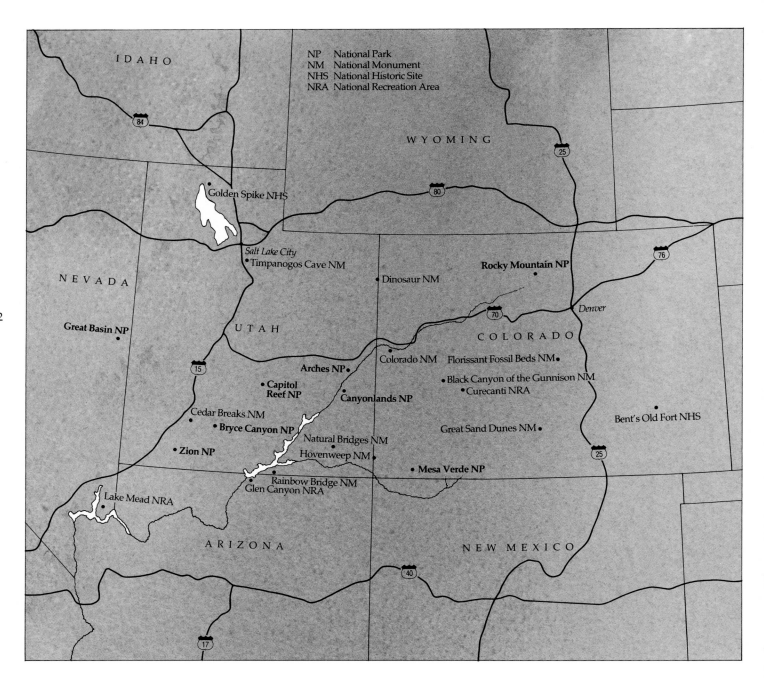

I D A H O

NP   National Park
NM   National Monument
NHS   National Historic Site
NRA   National Recreation Area

W Y O M I N G

Golden Spike NHS

Salt Lake City
Timpanogos Cave NM

N E V A D A

Dinosaur NM

Rocky Mountain NP

Denver

Great Basin NP

U T A H

C O L O R A D O

Colorado NM   Florissant Fossil Beds NM

Arches NP

Capitol Reef NP

Black Canyon of the Gunnison NM
Curecanti NRA

Canyonlands NP

Cedar Breaks NM

Bent's Old Fort NHS

Bryce Canyon NP

Natural Bridges NM

Great Sand Dunes NM

Zion NP

Hovenweep NM

Mesa Verde NP

Rainbow Bridge NM
Glen Canyon NRA

Lake Mead NRA

A R I Z O N A

N E W   M E X I C O

72

COLORADO, UTAH & NEVADA

ROCKY MOUNTAIN, MESA VERDE, ARCHES, CANYONLANDS, CAPITOL REEF, BRYCE CANYON, ZION & GREAT BASIN NATIONAL PARKS

If variety is the spice of the outdoor vacationer's life, consider for a moment the expansive region of the West covered by the states of Colorado, Utah and Nevada. Nowhere in the National Park System is there more variety in topography, geology, flora and fauna, land use or in the sheer number of sites large and small set aside for the wilderness, recreational or cultural enjoyment of present and future generations. In these three states, which cover nearly 300,000 square miles of mountains, deserts and tablelike plateaus, are eight national parks, more than in any other of the five regions of the West into which this book is divided. There are, in addition, nine other sites administered by the National Park Service: national monuments, national recreation areas, and areas preserved for their cultural and historic value.

The region includes America's most recent national park—Great Basin in eastern Nevada, established in 1986 as that state's first federal park—as well as two (Mesa Verde and Rocky Mountain, both in Colorado) that were created even before World War I, when the national park concept was still in its infancy.

But those are only numbers. More important to vacationers with differing tastes is the tremendous variety of opportunity that this cluster of outdoor oases represents. Topographically, they range from the treeless alpine heights of Rocky Mountain National Park, through which winds the loftiest paved road in the United States except for Alaska, to the water-sculpted, brilliantly colored, exquisite ridges, canyons, spires, arches and domes of desertlike Canyon Country of central and southern Utah.

Depending upon which way you look, here are verdant stands of firs and spruces thickly blanketing a hillside, or a desert landscape covered with dusty sagebrush. Here are tumbling waterfalls or bone dry alkali flats, desert-dwelling jackrabbits or meadow-grazing deer, cactus wrens or mountain quail.

To the high-altitude transcontinental jet passenger, the landscape below may seem a meaningless blur. To the land-bound visitor, given a bit of patience and time, a new surprise awaits just past each bend in the road. Around one corner, perhaps, lie the preserved cliff dwellings of an ancient Indian people, vanished even before Columbus waded ashore at San Salvador. Around another, a deep canyon whose precipitous walls have been etched to exquisite form over millions of years. Past another turn, a quiet lake, perhaps, a flower-covered meadow, or the embryo trickle of a river beginning its thousand mile journey to the sea.

Lumped together, the three states represent a little more than one fourth of the land area of the 11 states of the contiguous American West. There are more people here than in the Mountain North states of Idaho, Wyoming and Montana . . . but not many more. Even with a combined population now approaching the six million mark—due largely to the mushrooming growth in the Denver and Salt Lake City metropolitan areas—their population density (the average number of people per square mile) still hovers under 20. That's less than one third of the average of the United States as a whole, and, like the Mountain North spreading over them on the map, it means there is still a lot of wide open (and up and down) spaces here where the trees still outnumber the people by a wide margin.

Of the three states, Colorado, the most populous, is the second largest in size (after Nevada). It's a diverse state whose topography must be measured vertically as well as laterally, for Colorado is, in the minds of most people as well as in the lyrics of John Denver, a "Rocky Mountain High."

Even from that jetliner flying overhead at 35,000 feet, one simply cannot miss the Rocky Mountains of Colorado, whatever the season. Though this massive mountain chain extends all the way from Canada to Mexico, nowhere is it more impressive than in Colorado, where every one of its 54 peaks exceeding 14,000 feet in elevation has its foundation planted firmly in Colorado bedrock. There are 13 peaks in the United States taller than 14,431-foot-high Mount Elbert, Colorado's highest mountain, including Mount Whitney in California and 12 others in Alaska. But Colorado's *average* elevation of 6,800 feet well qualifies it as the nation's highest state, Alaska not excepted.

The product of tumultuous changes which have occurred in the earth over at least a billion years, the Rockies provide some of the most splendid scenery in America. Some of the splendor is preserved in 414-square-mile Rocky Moun-

tain National Park northwest of Denver. It is in this park, as in other sections of the Rockies, that one may see, study or photograph a wide range of life forms—animals as well as trees and other plants—as one ascends from the base of the mountains to their snow-clad peaks rising more than two miles in the clear Colorado sky.

The Continental Divide extends through a part of Colorado. Running the width of the United States, this meandering line dictates whether rain or snowmelt in the Centennial State will eventually wind up in the Pacific Ocean, the Gulf of California, the Gulf of Mexico or the Atlantic Ocean. The Colorado Rockies are the source of six large river systems. Five of them—the Arkansas, North Platte, South Platte, Republic and Rio Grande—flow eastward from the Continental Divide. The sixth system—the Colorado—starts 10,000 feet up in the Never Summer Mountains west of Denver and then flows 1,400 miles to the Gulf of California.

Surprising to many is Colorado's climate. For a state that reaches to such Alp-like heights it is, meteorologically speaking, a fairly dry state, in terms of both annual precipitation and relative humidity. It's also warmer here than many people realize; even in January, mile-high Denver temperatures are as high or higher than in any American city of the same latitude.

Statewide, Colorado precipitation averages only about 16 inches annually, about the same as Los Angeles. The combination of low humidity and high altitude is responsible for a powdery snow rather than the slushy kind—a fact which Colorado boosters happily discovered years ago when they built the first of

the state's 35 major ski resorts.

Another surprising discovery for many first-time visitors here is that, John Denver's praise notwithstanding, Colorado is not all Alps and pine trees. East of the Rockies, all the way to the Kansas and Nebraska borders, is where the American Great Plains begin. It's far more likely that you'll find cattle ranchers and sheepherders here than mountaineers and ski instructors. And to the west, past the opposite slope of the Rockies, the land drops away to plateau country which contains, among other natural and cultural points of interest, Mesa Verde National Park, established in 1906 to preserve valuable artifacts relating to the prehistoric Anasazi culture.

More than 22 million acres of Colorado are forested, including huge tracts in the western part of the state devoted to national forests. This suggests tremendous opportunities for camping, hiking, backpacking, fishing and bird and wildlife watching. Despite its low population density, Colorado's wilderness can, however, get a bit crowded in midsummer; Rocky Mountain National Park alone draws more than two million visitors a year, the busiest months being July and August. And especially in the Rockies' higher elevations, heavy snows shut down many wilderness and recreational sites (except, of course, the ski areas) in winter. That's all the more justification for planning your trip just after Labor Day, or in spring before the next season's rush begins.

In addition to the two national parks, there are six other National Park Service sites in Colorado, all but one of them located in the western half of the state. They, too, deserve consideration by off-season visitors.

74

Hovenweep National Monument, near Cortes in the southwestern corner of the state, preserves ruins of pre-Columbian Indian culture, as does nearby Yucca House National Monument. Although both are close to Mesa Verde National Park, only Hovenweep can be visited by the public. Yucca House, created in 1919, is still being excavated by archaeologists.

In Black Canyon of the Gunnison National Monument, near Montrose, you can drive along either rim of a sheer-walled chasm whose rocky origin is still a mystery. East of Montrose, on the highway to Gunnison, you'll find the 42,000-acre Curecanti National Monument which includes 11 miles of the Gunnison River and two high-country lakes: Crystal Lake and Morrow Point Lake.

There are more canyons to explore at Colorado National Monument, just south of Fruita, as well as weird-shaped sandstone formations sculpted by time and weather. About 100 miles due north of Fruita is Dinosaur National Monument, part of which lies in neighboring Utah. There are spectacular canyons here, too, cut by the Green and Yampa Rivers. But Dinosaur's major claim to fame is what its name implies: the fossil remains of many dinosaurs and other prehistoric animals, removed from a huge fossil pit called the Quarry. In summer, rangers give interpretive talks that relate the fossils to the period of earth's history they represent.

More of Colorado's ancient past can be seen at Florissant Fossil Beds National Monument, west of Colorado Springs. Here has been unearthed and preserved a wealth of fossils ranging from insects to seeds and leaves—plus a group of petrified sequoia stumps which indicate that this species of tree, now found only in California, was once distributed over a much larger area of the North American continent. Trails out of Florissant lead to splendid views of Pike's Peak, the old gold-mining town of Cripple Creek, and golden eagles soaring high above. And, 37 miles northeast of Alamosa in south-central Colorado, is Great Sand Dunes National Monument, where are found the tallest dunes in the United States. They were formed over thousands of years as winds swept down from the Sangre de Cristo Mountains.

Utah is another state of widely varying topography and natural beauty. Covering 84,961 square miles, it includes several landforms: part of the large, high Colorado Plateau; part of the Middle Rockies running east-west in the northeast corner; the wildlife-rich Wasatch Range lying east of Salt Lake City and the Great Salt Lake itself; the eastern portion of the Great Basin; great expanses of alkali salt flats; and, in the southeast section referred to as the Four Corners region, the stark, breathtakingly beautiful Canyon Country.

Utah is home to five national parks, five national monuments, two federally designated historic sites, and the Glen Canyon National Recreation Area; a huge swath of its north-south middle is devoted to national forests as well. To the benefit of the Utah vacationer, most of the park sites are clustered in the central and southern part of the state, mainly in Canyon Country where nature has fashioned a magnificent landscape of plateaus, canyons and brilliantly colored rock formations that dazzle the eye and pique the imagination. Part of Canyon Country spills over the border into Arizona and, by the definition of some, it includes the greatest canyon of them all, the Grand Canyon.

Utah's Canyon Country is one of the largest wilderness areas of North America south of Canada. Though it is served by modern highways, parts of it even today cannot be reached except on foot, horseback, four-wheel-drive vehicle, or by boat along the Colorado and Green Rivers. Parts are high and wooded. In summer, that's a blessing, because the lower plateaus and canyons sizzle in July and August. Below 6,000 feet in elevation, only about 10 inches of precipitation occur annually. In summer, some of it comes in the form of violent thunderstorms; in winter, as snow flurries.

Almost any kind and shape of rock formation can be found here, some singly and some, as in Bryce Canyon and Zion National Parks, in huge clusters. There are literally thousands of rocks: pinnacles, spires, serpentine ridges, natural bridges, domes, plateaus and, strangest of all, the scalloped pieces the ancient people called "hoodoos."

Canyon Country was formed by many geological factors: uplift, some volcanism, a lot of erosion by water. The story of this formation, a fascinating one, is best told in the exhibits, talks and specialized publications available at the park and monument visitor centers.

Central Utah—the hub of population around Salt Lake City—is the world capital of the Mormon Church. North of the capital, near Ogden, is Snow Basin, one of the Beehive State's many fine ski areas. Though their respective chambers of commerce may argue the point, many snow buffs now rate Utah superior to Colorado. Both states, because of ideal powder-on-hardbase snow conditions, offer the finest skiing in the nation.

Utah shares with its neighbor, Nevada, the large landform known as the Great Basin. Starting just east of the Sierra Nevada and Cascade mountain ranges, the Great Basin has been variously called a "wasteland," "worthless" or, a bit more poetically, "a painfully lonely vastness." That all depends upon your point of view. If you have ever driven eastward into Nevada after leaving the verdant wonderland of the Sierra or the Cascades, the miles and miles of sagebrush may turn you off cold. Certainly, the geography seems a little destitute here, and even the rivers don't act as rivers are supposed to. In this basin, not a single stream flows anywhere but within the basin itself, either evaporating or settling into "sinks" like Utah's Bonneville salt flats. Not a drop flows to the ocean, where all rivers are supposed to flow. Yet in the great, flat, stark, almost featureless void that is the Great Basin, a surprising amount of life does indeed exist, and for the scientifically curious, it merits exploration.

It may be appropriate, therefore, that the nation's newest national park—Great Basin, just outside the town of Baker, Nevada, near the Utah border—has focused attention on this oft-misunderstood region of Western America. Contrasted to the "painfully lonely vastness" that some parts of the Great Basin seem to represent, its cool mountain country holds a few surprises for those who have always thought of Nevada only in terms of casinos, Hoover Dam and a dumping ground for nuclear waste.

Rocky Mountain National Park

Trail Ridge Road in Rocky Mountain National Park is one of the great alpine highways of the United States. At one point in its 50-mile meander east-west and then north-south through the 414 square miles of this Colorado park, it reaches an altitude of 12,183 feet, making it the highest (in elevation) paved road in the contiguous 48 states. Human lungs strain for oxygen at this elevation. Car engines, tuned at sea level, lug at reduced efficiency. Warm clothes are a must, and hypothermia—loss of body heat through exposure—is of real concern.

But to anyone who has driven Trail Ridge Road its full length, or, better yet, hiked the 16-mile (round trip) trail to the summit of 14,255-foot-high Longs Peak, the reward is one of the most superb high-mountain experiences in America.

Located in the north-central Colorado highlands, the snow-covered peaks of Rocky Mountain National Park climb above verdant alpine valleys and jewel-like lakes. Much of the park is forested—ponderosa pine, juniper and Douglas fir are common trees depending upon the area and elevation—but some of it is not. More than one third of Rocky Mountain is above the tree line, one of the reasons its subalpine and alpine grandeur was preserved as a national park shortly after the turn of the century. In the alpine tundra are plants, adapted to living at harsh, high altitudes, stunted and fragile. Their growing season may be as short as 10 weeks; some are as small as a dime. More than one-fourth of the plants you see here are also found in the Arctic; hence, Rocky Mountain National Park represents in a microcosm a segment of what one would find in the Arctic north but preserved here within relatively easy access of millions of people.

In terms of visitors, Rocky Mountain rivals Wyoming's Yellowstone and California's Yosemite in terms of peak season crowding. About 2½ million people are drawn to Rocky Mountain every year, most of them during the summer months when park visitation traditionally is at its statistical peak. Off-season, visiting drops off dramatically. But although many roads and trails are closed by snow during the Rocky Mountain winter, activities in this season are many, including both cross-country and downhill skiing, snowmobiling (in restricted areas), snowshoeing, camping and backcountry hiking. Fall and spring—nearly as uncrowded as winter—are profitable visiting times, too. In fall, visitors may witness the golden display of quaking aspens or hear the bugling of an elk in rut. In spring, wildflowers put on a show of their own, the various species blooming in seasonal succession as one climbs from the lower valleys to the high country. There are many species, including the exquisite blue columbine, Colorado's state flower.

It was in 1859 that Joel Estes and his son, Milton, rode through this area. Many landmarks now bear their name, including the town of Estes Park. Not until around 1900, however, did settlers begin to arrive in any substantial number. One of them, a naturalist, writer and conservationist named Enos Mills, was so impressed he began a campaign to preserve the region for future generations. Mills's efforts bore fruit when Rocky Mountain was accorded national park status by Congress in 1915.

The main entrance to Rocky Mountain

is about 2½ miles west of the mountain town of Estes Park, which in turn is 65 miles northwest of the Denver urban area. Park headquarters is located just before the entrance. This center and another, on the opposite side of the park, near Grand Lake, are open year-round; two additional centers, Moraine Park Museum and Alpine Visitor Center, are open during the late spring through fall peak visitor period only. There is no lodging anywhere in the park, although many motels and hotels are available both in Estes Park and Grand Lake, with most of them remaining open throughout the year.

By auto, Trail Ridge Road provides a good sampling of what this park is all about, its plant and animal communities, and a crossing of the Continental Divide at Milner Pass, 10,758 feet high. The road is usually open from Memorial Day to mid-October, depending upon snowfall. That leaves plenty of time to drive it before midsummer crowds form, or after visitors leave. On Trail Ridge Road, you are literally on the roof of the Rockies. From overlooks such as the one at Forest Canyon, you'll have superb vistas of glacier-carved peaks. Features of the alpine tundra—at once fragile and tenacious— are explained in exhibits at the Alpine Visitor Center near Fall River Pass.

Rounding the many switchbacks on the road, you'll appreciate how tough it was to thread an auto path through these rugged mountains. Past Fall River Pass, Trail Ridge Road then turns southwest and south in its path through Kawuneeche Valley on its way to Grand Lake, on the western boundary of the park. Never Summer Ranch and Lulu City are located a short hike from this portion of the road.

Joe Arnold

HALLETT PEAK, *12,713 feet high, and Flattop Mountain, reaching 12,324 feet, dominate this winter snow scene in Rocky Mountain National Park, Colorado.*

If you want a feel for what traveling in these mountains was like before Trail Ridge Road, try the Fall River Road which runs from Horseshoe Park Junction to Fall River Pass. From Endovalley northwestward, the paved road ends and a gravel road begins. Vehicles may travel only one way—upward—to the end of this road near the Alpine Visitor Center, and no trailers or vehicles over 25 feet long are allowed.

Another scenic tour is Bear Lake Road. Leading from the Moraine Park Museum to Bear Lake at its terminus are many trails leading up the eastern slope of the Rockies toward the Continental Divide. Driving this road, one learns again the value of off-season national park visiting. In midsummer, parking lots at both Bear Lake, located in the heart of a high mountain basin, and at nearby Glacier Gorge Junction, are usually full between 10 A.M. and 3 P.M. You won't have any parking problems if you tour the park in a commercial sightseeing bus (in season) or use the shuttle bus inside the park, but for private cars, traffic jams can be a very real problem in summer.

Rocky Mountain is a splendid park for the hiker. It's even a park where the handicapped visitor can enjoy wilderness; the Sprague Lake "Five Senses Trail," one-half mile long and level, is accessible for wheelchairs. There are 355 miles of trail in Rocky Mountain, ranging from short, easy strolls just off the roadway, to more arduous, high-altitude climbs that require a full day or more. Regardless of trail length, allow more time for hiking here than in parks at lower elevation. Even if you are in top physical condition, exhaustion can occur quickly.

Here are just a few samples of hiking opportunities available:

At Bear Lake, a one-half mile trail, 9,475 feet in elevation, leads to a close-up look at the lake's many features. A fine cross section of Rocky Mountain's many plant and animal communities can be appreciated in an even shorter (one quarter mile) stroll around Moraine Park. It's at 8,000 feet in elevation. There are a number of short trails leading to the tundra region from the Rock Cut and Forest Canyon overlooks, southwest of the Alpine Visitor Center on Trail Ridge Road. They are at various elevations from 11,600 to 12,310 feet.

For the more ambitious, the Wild Basin Trail leads to sections of the park marked by glaciated valleys, streams and

77

Joe Arnold

THE SEASONS *can change quickly—and spectacularly—in Rocky Mountain National Park, Colorado. On these pages are depicted some natural symbols of those changes. From left to right: snow patches cover the Petit Crepon and Sharkstooth area as viewed from Sky Pond; wild iris herald the arrival of spring; the yellows and golds of aspen, a fall spectacle, contrast with the more somber appearance of boulders near Bear Lake; ground-hugging plants cling to life in the*

Joe Arnold

Joe Arnold

Rocky Mountain tundra of the park's higher elevations. In the two-page photograph are Otis Peak, Hallett Peak and Flattop Mountain, reflected in Sprague Lake. By moving from the lowest elevation in the park to the highest, one may experience an extreme range of nature in terms of both wildlife and plants. Generally speaking, plant communities are densest at lower levels, reduced both in size and growing season higher up. Those in the tundra region, a harsh, fragile zone usually associated with the arctic, are a special world all their own.

Joe Arnold

waterfalls. Extending 16 miles, it ranges from 8,470 to 11,000 feet in elevation.

For serious hikers, though, the 16-mile climb to Longs Peak, Rocky Mountain's highest point, is the ultimate experience in a visit to this park. The trail, climbing nearly one mile in elevation (from 9,554 to 14,255 feet), leads to superb subalpine forests, tundra and glacial landscapes.

In summer, many trails are heavily used. If you don't enjoy crowds in the wilderness, park rangers will suggest lesser-used ones; both trail guides and topographic maps—the latter a definite aid on the longer trails—are available at visitor centers.

Climbers at Rocky Mountain will find many challenging ascents, and both guide service and mountaineering instruction are offered in season. There are regulations governing mountaineering; checking with a ranger in advance will assure a more rewarding and safer climb. Longs Peak can be reached by climbers as well as hikers; in July, August and part of September, a route through the Keyhole can be followed even without technical climbing equipment.

As many an early explorer or settler learned, the high Rockies demand respect from the human intruder. Their beauty can mask danger, and visitors should be prepared for both sudden weather changes and hazards of the terrain. Streams and waterfalls are spectacular in spring, for instance, but the same rushing turbulence that pleases the eye can be downright dangerous to the wader or swimmer. Thunderstorms dazzle, but the lightning they contain can be lethal; ridges and lone objects such as large rocks and trees should be avoided during storms. The same precautions apply to wildlife; though grizzly bears (which Rocky Mountain does not have) may have a more ferocious reputation, black bears (which it does) are just as wild and should be left alone.

Heeding the safety rules, Rocky Mountain, a park for nearly every outdoor taste, can be a thoroughly rewarding experience. Horseback riding is popular here; guides can be hired at two locations. So is fishing, although high altitude and cold waters nurture fish that are too small for many anglers' satisfaction (Rocky Mountain's four trout species are the German brown, rainbow, brook and cutthroat).

In winter, there is downhill skiing in Hidden Valley, seven miles from the Beaver Meadows entrance. Winter backpacking and camping are permitted, but areas prone to avalanches should be avoided. The Aspenglen, Longs Peak and Timber Creek campgrounds are open all year, and there is no camping fee. There are nearly 800 campsites altogether in the park, including those at trail camps, for which permits are required.

Rocky Mountain National Park Estes Park, CO 80517, (303) 586-2371
Access: By auto: from Estes Park on the east, via U.S. 34/36; via Trail Ridge Road; from the southwest via U.S. 34 to Grand Lake. Trail Ridge Road closed from mid-October to Memorial Day. Commercial bus tours within park.
Season: Park open all year. Trail Ridge Road and Old Fall River Road usually closed in October. Park headquarters visitor center closed Dec. 25.
Visitor Centers: At park headquarters west of Estes Park; Kawuneeche, near Grand Lake entrance (both year-round); Alpine and Moraine Park, summer only.
Lodging: In park: none. For information on lodging near the park, write the Chamber of Commerce at either Estes Park, CO 80517, or Grand Lake, CO 80447.
Camping: Five roadside campgrounds at Moraine Park, Glacier Basin, Timber Creek, Long Peak and Aspenglen (June–September). Campgrounds usually fill up early in day, some time restrictions. No showers, electrical, water or sewage connections in any campground. Reservations for Moraine Park and Glacier Basin campgrounds available through Ticketron during the summer. Privately owned camping facilities available outside the park.
Services: In park: light lunches available at Trail Ridge Store (Fall River Pass) in summer, at Hidden Valley Winter Use Area in winter. No other food or supplies available in park. Food and supplies at Estes and Grand Lake, near the park.
Activities: Auto touring, hiking (355 miles of trails), mountain climbing, fishing, horseback riding, downhill and cross-country skiing, snowshoeing, snowmobiling (west side only), bird and animal watching, guided walks, interpretive programs, campfire programs in season. Backpacking; overnight stay requires permit.

For further information on permits, fees, reservations and park regulations, write or call park headquarters.

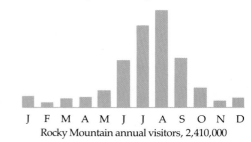
J F M A M J J A S O N D
Rocky Mountain annual visitors, 2,410,000

80

THE DISCOVERY of Cliff Palace in 1888, largest ruin in Mesa Verde National Park, launched the campaign which led to the establishment of the park. The ruin is located on Chapin Mesa.

Tom Bean

Mesa Verde National Park

Nine centuries before Columbus discovered the New World, a group of Indians selected a high, verdant tableland in present-day Colorado for their new home. The plateau, in the Four Corners area of the state, is called Mesa Verde. The settlers were known as the Anasazi—Navajo for "ancient ones."

Working in harmony with nature, the Anasazi built their dwellings under the overhanging cliffs. Their basic material was sandstone, shaped in rectangular blocks about the size of a bread loaf. Mud and water served as mortar. Rooms, about six feet by eight, were large enough for two or three people and much of the daily routine in the village took place in the open courtyards in front of these rooms.

Formerly a nomadic people, the earliest Anasazi were known as Basketmakers because of their adeptness at this craft. Life was simple, and it was, for a while, prosperous. Later, homebuilding became more permanent; about 750 A.D., the Anasazi began fashioning their dwellings above ground with upright walls of poles and mud. From this period on, they had a new name: Pueblos, the Spanish word for village dwellers.

Then, inexplicably, the Anasazi began to vanish from Mesa Verde, and they were gone within the span of only one or two generations in the late 1200s.

Mesa Verde National Park was established in 1906 to preserve the remnants of this culture, considered to be the most noteworthy preservation of its kind in the United States. So rugged is the area that it was passed up by early white explorers; it was only by chance that the Anasazi ruins were discovered in the 19th Century.

81

Federal protection of the plateau, rising high above the Mancos and Montezuma Valleys of southwest Colorado, put a halt to vandalism which had begun to desecrate some of the sites. The discovery of Mesa Verde's ruins also stirred interest in knowing more about these ancient people: how they lived, what they ate, what crops they grew, and, the thorniest riddle of them all, why they abandoned what seemed to be an ideal, protected, well-knit community.

Today's visitor to Mesa Verde will find not only well-preserved examples of the Anasazi cliff homes, but also many artifacts relating to their culture: pottery, tools, baskets, utensils and weapons.

The visitor center at Far View, 17 miles inside the park entrance off U.S. 160, has many exhibits on the Anasazi culture. The center is open only in summer. Another worthwhile starting point is the Chapin Mesa Archaeological Museum, 21 miles from the entrance, open all year.

Exhibits at both centers preserve the arts and crafts of both the prehistoric (pre-Columbian) and historic Indians of the region. Roadside exhibits interpret the cliff dwellings and other ruins, and there are outlooks where the entire community may be seen.

Tours of Wetherill Mesa at the southwestern corner of the park are available during the summer months. Private autos have been allowed from Far View to Wetherill Mesa since 1987. Two cliff dwellings, Step House and Long House, and four mesa-top villages, are open to the public. It's a strenuous hike to the cliff dwellings from the road, and at altitudes ranging from 6,000 to 8,500 feet, not one for the weak of heart. All major cliff dwellings can be viewed from overlooks, however.

Cliff Palace on Chapin Mesa is the largest ruin in the park. Its discovery in 1888 led to extensive archaeological explorations and the campaign to establish the national park.

Though Mesa Verde is primarily a cultural park, there are limited camping facilities and hiking trails here, and in winter, cross-country skiing and snowshoeing are permitted.

A short trail leads hikers from Chapin Mesa to the Spruce Tree House ruin. The visitor standing across the canyon from this village, the only ruin open in winter, may well imagine what life was like here before Columbus. One of the largest in Mesa Verde, the village had 114 rooms and eight kivas (ceremonial rooms, the Anasazi equivalent of the modern church). About 100 to 125 Anasazi lived here, their activities varying from season to season. When the Anasazi left, they may have migrated south into New Mexico or Arizona. Some of today's Pueblo Indians of these states may be the Anasazi's descendants.

In summer, daytime temperatures in the park are warm, comfortable and dry, with a range of 85–100 degrees F; evenings are cool, ranging from 55–65. Winter is cold, with considerable snow.

Overnight accommodations are available outside the park at Cortez and Mancos, seven and eight miles from the entrance, respectively. The only in-park, noncamping accommodations are at the Far View Lodge, a 150-unit hostelry operated by a concessioner from early May to mid-October. Located at 8,000 feet, the lodge affords a sweeping view from each room of three states: Colorado, New Mexico and Arizona. Mule deer frequently wander the grounds. There are no telephones or TVs in the rooms, but

their absence should disturb few visitors. After all, the ancient Anasazi got along here quite well without them, long, long ago.

Mesa Verde National Park Mesa Verde National Park, CO 81330, (303) 529-4465
Access: By auto: 7 miles east from Cortez or 8 miles west from Mancos, Colorado, via Hwy. 160. By air: Trans-Colorado Airlines serves Cortez.
Season: Park open all year. Wetherill Mesa accessible only during summer months. All roads hazardous in winter.
Visitor Centers: Far View Visitor Center (summer only, 8 A.M. to 5 P.M.), Chapin Mesa Museum, open all year.
Lodging: In park: Far View Lodge, open mid-May to mid-October; reservations advised June 1 to Labor Day, write or phone the Mesa Verde Co., P.O. Box 227, Mancos, CO 81328, (303) 529-4421. Nearby: at Mancos or Cortez, CO.
Camping: Morefield campground open mid-April to mid-October for tents, RVs, and trailers. No reservations accepted.
Services: In park: gasoline, food, supplies, meals, at Far View and Morefield Village; food at Chapin Mesa and Wetherill Mesa mid-May to mid-October only. Nearby: at Mancos and Cortez, CO.
Activities: Driving, hiking, cross-country skiing and snowshoeing, photography, guided tours, limited biking, ranger talks and religious programs in summer.

For further information on permits, fees, reservations or park regulations, call or write park headquarters.

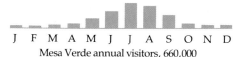

Mesa Verde annual visitors, 660,000

PARK VISITORS *use a ladder to reach the Long House Ruin, located on Wetherill Mesa. It has a large central plaza that in ancient times was used for dances and village ceremonies.*

Tom Bean

Arches National Park

Nature has sculpted rock arches large and small in many places throughout the world. No place, however, has so many arches so varied in size and design as in Arches National Park, located in southeast Utah's vivid red rock country.

The product of more than 100 million years of violent forces, there are more than 500 arches and rock forms of all kinds here: pinnacles, rock windows and pedestals, all constantly changing color as light shifts throughout the day. They range in size from arches only 3 feet in diameter (the official minimum for measurement) to Landscape Arch, 105 feet high and 291 feet from base to base.

The full range of arch-building and decay, spanning centuries, can be seen from convenient roadside vantage points, or on short hiking trails. Some of the formations seem so sturdily anchored, they appear rooted forever; others, delicately balanced, appear ready to topple at any moment. So varied are the arches in the Windows Section, reached by a spur road off the main park road, early explorers wondered if they might be man-made wonders of an earlier culture, like the famous Stonehenge of England.

Exhibits at the park's visitor center near the entrance portray in detail the fascinating story of how these rock formations came to be. Briefly, however, they are creations of many geologic processes: the ebb and flow of an ancient sea that once buried the Colorado Plateau, of battering by floods and winds, of buckling, shifting and liquefaction under tremendous pressures from within the earth's crust.

The arches at one point in their development were solid rock. Fins (or ridges), formed by uplifting and faulting, became arches when alternating frosts and thawing, among other forces, gnawed away at their midsections until they caved in. In time, many of these arches will further erode, leaving only pillars or pinnacles.

A self-guiding auto tour booklet, available at the visitor center, will help you budget your time during a visit. In spring, summer and fall, naturalists conduct a two-hour Fiery Furnace Walk and other guided hikes, covering many points of interest.

Bring your camera; you'll keep it busy. The balanced rocks, spires and eroded fins of Park Avenue, for instance, resemble a city skyline. The huge monoliths of Sheep Rock and Three Gossips, and a small arch still in the making, comprise Courthouse Towers. The four large arches of the Windows Section are visible at camera range from the roadway. And from Panorama Point, you'll have a sweeping view of Salt Valley and Fiery Furnace—particularly spectacular at sunset.

If time permits, extend your visit to include Canyonlands National Park, north and south of Arches, Deadhorse Point or Dinosaur and Natural Bridges National Monuments and the Glen Canyon National Recreation Area. The old Mormon town of Moab, five miles south of Arches, is worth a visit; in the 1940s and 1950s, it enjoyed a brief, prosperous boom as a uranium mining center.

Many features of Arches National Park can be seen from the main road which extends 18 miles from the entrance to Devil's Garden, where camping is available.

There are many hiking trails and self-guided tours here, and backpacking is allowed with a permit. Carrying water is a must, especially in summer, when temperatures often soar over 100 degrees F. Winters are mild; snow patches on the red rock are beautiful.

Spring and fall are excellent times for a visit, the best times of all, in the opinion of many. Wildflowers bloom in profusion from May to August, and wildlife here is typical of that found throughout the Great Basin desert.

Arches National Park P.O. Box 907, Moab, UT 84532, (801) 259-8161
Access: By auto: 5 miles north of Moab, Utah, on U.S. 191.
Season: Park open all year.
Visitor Center: At park headquarters, off U.S. 191 at park entrance.
Lodging: In park: none. Nearby: in Moab, Utah, 5 miles southeast of park entrance.
Camping: At Devil's Garden, 18 miles north of Visitor Center, fee season March–October; no reservations accepted; free camping but no water rest of year; 53 campsites.
Services: In park: No meals or supplies. Nearby: in Moab, Utah. Restrooms at Visitor Center.
Activities: Hiking (brochures available at Visitor Center), backpacking by permit, exhibits.

For further information on permits, fees, reservations and park regulations, write or call park headquarters.

J F M A M J J A S O N D
Arches annual visitors, 420,000

Pat O'Hara

NORTH WINDOW *Arch, at left, is one of four water-eroded formations in Arches National Park, Utah. At right, Landscape Arch, another favorite with visitors, sprinkled with snow. Delicate Arch, bottom, was so named because of its fragile appearance. However, it's unlikely to topple for a long time.*

Pat O'Hara

85

Pat O'Hara

86

Pat O'Hara

THE COLORADO RIVER *meanders through Canyonlands National Park, Utah, as seen in this view from Deadhorse Point State Park. Bypassed by many early immigrants because of its remoteness, the Canyonlands region is testimony to the work of wind, sun and harsh seasons.*

Canyonlands National Park

Nineteenth Century geologist-explorer John Wesley Powell once described Utah's rock-ribbed Canyonland country as "grandeur, glory and desolation . . . all merged into one." He went on to call it "a strange, weird, grand region . . . a landscape everywhere . . . of rock." Few of today's visitors to Canyonlands National Park could improve upon Powell's words; the dictionary simply doesn't contain enough adjectives to sum up what most people feel about this 527-square-mile, laid-bare backbone of the American continent when they view it for the first or the hundredth time.

Canyonlands is not a national park that is easy to visit, where a quick drive-through in a car will provide intimate details at a glance. It requires a bit of work. Parts of the park in fact demand a four-wheel drive vehicle, and there are other corners that until very recently saw almost no humans at all since the days when the ancient Anasazi lived here, leaving a record of their activities in fascinating cliffside etchings.

Located between and to the west of Moab and Monticello, Utah, Canyonlands includes the confluence of two important Western rivers—the Colorado and the Green—as well as some of the most spectacular, isolated, varied rock formations on the continent.

Within Canyonlands are two major canyons and several smaller ones, rock spires and mesas that rise to 7,800 feet, monoliths, arches, a sweeping vista of the La Sal, Abajo and Henry Mountains, an ever-shifting kaleidoscope of color. Desolate, remote, inaccessible: these are words used by early explorers that might equally be applied to Canyonlands today. Little wonder that most 19th Century, westward-moving migrants by-passed this inhospitable section of Utah, and that the region seemed so unattractive even to despoilers that it did not become a national park until 1964.

Canyonlands is divided into three distinct geological districts, four, if you count, as some scientists do, the section directly influenced by the two rivers. The most remote part of the park is the Maze, west of the Colorado and Green Rivers, a region of spectacular buttes, broken rock and weird-shaped stone towers. The Maze contains Horseshoe Canyon, whose so-called Great Gallery of reproductions of life-sized figures, is considered one of the finest examples of prehistoric rock art. They are thought to have been painted by Fremont Indians, predecessors of the Anasazi, or "Ancient Ones."

There are few trails in the Maze and where they do exist, hiking is tough. Especially in the swelter of summer, the district is best left to the serious, experienced hiker with proper backpack and an adequate supply of water. But for the visitor who is well prepared, here is some of Canyonlands' most rewarding wilderness landscape.

Rising between the Colorado and the Green Rivers, the Island in the Sky district is a towering rock mesa which affords a 3,000-foot-high view of the rivers and the landscape below. It is easily accessible, thanks to a new paved road.

Perhaps the most picturesque district is the Needles, an area of massive sandstone spires, rock needles, arches and pinnacles given such appropriate names as Devil's Kitchen and Angel Arch. There are many trails here, and a four-wheel-drive vehicle is helpful; the rocky road up Elephant Hill, providing vehicle entry to the Needles interior, will test any four-wheeler to its limit.

Canyonlands visitation follows the usual national park annual cycle except that there is a marked drop-off in July and August before rising again in September and October. A glance at the thermometer shows why. Cool and comfortable in late fall, winter and spring, Canyonlands sizzles in midsummer, with many days topping 100 degrees F; the total annual rainfall averages only about 10 inches.

If you are neither hiker nor four-wheeler, there are concessioner-operated tours of the park in well-equipped Land Rovers, in season. Spring wildflowers are impressive, and snow is possible in winter.

Except for campgrounds, there are no lodging, food or supplies available in Canyonlands. Nor is Canyonlands conveniently located along any major route to anywhere. Off the beaten track, lacking most of the comforts of home, a desolate land that explorer John Macomb described simply as "an impracticable region," for the seeker of solitude and primitive geological beauty, Canyonlands National Park is a rare treat.

Canyonlands National Park 125 W. 2nd South, Moab, UT 84532, (801) 259-7164
Access: By auto: 15 miles north of Monticello, Utah. Needles district on Utah 211, then 35 miles west on U.S. 191; Island in the Sky, 12 miles north of Moab on U.S. 191 then 23 miles southwest on Utah 313; Maze district 45 miles east of Utah 24 via dirt road.
Season: Park open all year. From October to mid-March, snow possible, roads can become impassable.
Visitor Centers: Contact stations for in-

formation in Needles, Island in the Sky and Maze districts. Maps, publications also available at park headquarters in Moab and the Monticello information center.

Lodging: In park: none. Nearby: Monticello, 50 miles; Moab, 35 miles; Green River, 60 miles.

Camping: Two campgrounds: Squaw Flat-Needles District, 26 sites; Willow Flat-Island District, 38 campsites. No reservations. Numerous backcountry primitive sites.

Services: In park: none. Food and supplies available in Monticello, Moab, Green River, Hanksville.

Activities: Boating, rafting, backpacking, hiking, auto and guided tours, horseback riding, mountain biking, concessioner-operated Jeep tours and Jeep rentals nearby.

For further information on permits, fees, reservations and park regulations, write or call park headquarters.

88

J F M A M J J A S O N D
Canyonlands annual visitors, 175,000

ROCK WALLS *of Green River Canyon are reflected in the Green River in this early morning photograph in Canyonlands National Park. Not as well known, perhaps, as the Colorado, the Green River was an important factor in forming Canyonlands' features.*

Pat O'Hara

GEOLOGY: HOW THE SOUTH-WEST BEGAN. *Driving through the Western states of Colorado, Utah and Nevada is like passing through a vast geological museum whose exhibits are the rocks, plateaus, mountains, deserts and canyons dating back more than 300 million years. They are in effect a* living *museum, since the earth-shaping processes they represent are continuing even today, though so imperceptibly they go unnoticed when measured against the span of a human lifetime.*

At almost every bend of the road, you'll see examples of the many processes: the uplifted, fault-block backbone of middle America we call the Rocky Mountains; rocks, in places like Utah's Zion and Bryce Canyon National Parks, that were sculpted into a thousand bizarre shapes and sizes by centuries of erosive wind and water; canyons gnawed deep and wide by rivers; peaks thrust skyward by volcanism; valleys carved by the glacier giants of the Ice Age.

Much of the evidence of this earth building is seen in national parks and monuments of the West. If geology interests you, most park visitor centers have special exhibits and displays on the subject.

You may want to purchase a few basic books and booklets which are also available in the parks. In addition, rangers are well versed on geologic history, and will be happy to answer questions you may have.

Geology can be complicated, but how it applies in the Rocky Mountain West can be divided into five or six simple "chapters," each spanning millions of years.

More than 300 million years ago, most of the West was covered by a vast, shallow sea, its surface broken only by a few hills and low-lying plains. Wind and water gradually wore down some of these peaks, but another group of mountains, known as the Ancestral Rockies, began to rise from the same sea in a chain that extended from Wyoming to Texas. About 230 million years ago, the eastern floor of the sea was tilted by gigantic forces within the earth. The climate became tropical in na-

BLUE MESA *near the center of Petrified National Park in Arizona typifies some of the geology found in the American Southwest. These are the so-called Pedestal Logs in the badlands section of the park.*

ture, and dinosaurs flourished. Although the soft sandstone and limestone materials that built these earliest Rockies can be found even today, the mountains themselves were almost completely worn away by erosion by about 160 million years ago.

Then occurred a period that geologists call the Laramide Revolution, lasting about 100 million years. More mountain building occurred as the crust of the earth, weakened and strained by the great weight of the ancient sea, began to buckle and fold upward.

By the time the Laramide Revolution ended, about 60 million years ago, this entire portion of the continent had risen above water, never to sink again.

Next, volcanoes added their fury to the process which, as evidenced by the geysers and hot springs of Yellowstone National Park, continues to a lesser extent even today. Much older clues to volcanism can be seen in rock formations like Devils Tower in Wyoming, 865 feet high, designated a national monument in 1906—first in the nation.

Finally, there were the glaciers. You'll see their handiwork here, too, in the distinctive canyons, valleys and plateaus sculpted by their tremendously heavy, slowly moving forms during the Ice Ages.

89

Tom Bean

Capitol Reef National Park

Millions of years of earth's history in the form of a spectacular, water-carved landscape can be appreciated in a drive or hike through Capitol Reef National Park in south-central Utah.

Established as a national monument in 1937, Capitol Reef was expanded and redesignated as a national park in 1971. It lies in Utah's slickrock country where over the eons water has carved monoliths, buttes, arches and mazes of canyons out of a shale and sandstone desert.

"Reef" means a ridge or barrier. Unlike those in tropical seas where they are usually of living coral, those in this park are of rock, laid down, layer by layer, in ages past. The park was named for Capitol Dome, one of its most prominent points, which resembles the dome of the U.S. Capitol in Washington, D.C.

Rugged, dry desert country that was first explored only a century ago, Capitol Reef is still largely a wilderness. It seems as if only yesterday Robert Leroy Parker (alias Butch Cassidy) passed through the area with his notorious Wild Bunch.

Except for campsites, there are no visitor accommodations, and no services such as food, supplies and gasoline. However, these are available not many miles outside the park at Torrey, Utah, and other towns.

The park is laid out long and very narrow; only in the northern end, between the Utah towns of Torrey and Caineville, is there a paved road—Utah State Hwy. 24. There are several pull-outs along Hwy. 24 from which it is only a short stroll to points of interest. For instance, you'll pass through Fruita, a former Mormon settlement whose last residents left in the late 1960s. The old Fruita schoolhouse has been preserved.

Also to be seen are petroglyphs—carvings in rock—left by the Fremont Indians as long ago as 400 A.D.

Paiute Indians hunted in Capitol Reef after the Fremonts left (possibly due to drought), but mainly as itinerant hunters and plant gatherers. The Mormons, whose trek to the Salt Lake Valley from Illinois in the mid-1800s was an important part of Western history, arrived and settled Fruita about 1880.

South and north of Hwy. 24, you'll be on dirt and gravel roads. A high clearance vehicle is necessary on some; four-wheel drive is helpful on a few. Yet it is on these unpaved roads along which some of Capitol Reef's finest scenery lies. Along Scenic Drive (gravel, about 25 miles round trip), for instance, you'll get breathtaking glimpses of the park's massive cliffs, and of Grand Wash and Capitol Gorge, two of the places where water has cut completely through the reef.

Dirt roads meander through the north end of the park. They lead through the heart of Cathedral Valley and along the rim to South Desert.

The south end of the park is good hiking country. The dirt road access to the south end is from Notom, once a farming community and now the site of three private ranches, just outside the park on the eastern side. The road parallels the park's eastern boundary for a while, then returns inside for a few miles, then exits again on its way to Bullfrog Marina and the Glen Canyon National Recreation Area. Excellent daylong or overnight hikes are possible along this route.

The southern region offers some spectacular scenery and more evidence of the forces that shaped this section of the earth's landscape. South of Notom, rock tilts to between 45 and 70 degrees on the east side of the Reef. Several washes make excellent day hiking trips here.

Capitol Reef is located on the Colorado Plateau, one of the West's largest and most important landforms. It was toward the end of the Age of Dinosaurs that the plateau and the Rocky Mountains began rising to their present height, folding and warping into fantastic shapes and formations.

Though the part of the park away from the Fremont River is desert, a sharp eye will spot a surprising number of animals—both birds and mammals—as well as plant life. Squirrels and chipmunks scurry everywhere. Fox, mountain lion and deer, less numerous, can best be seen at dawn, dusk or after dark. Pinyon pine and juniper, tenaciously adapting to the desert environment, grow wherever they can; along the Fremont River, by contrast, trees and shrubs grow in thick stands.

Capitol Reef, uncrowded in summer, is an even more ideal destination off-season. Fall foliage along the Fremont River is dazzling. Winter photography is superb. In spring, wildflowers break the desert monotony. And, best of all to many visitors, pesky insects seem to disappear when summer's crowds do.

Be wary of weather changes, however. Located about a mile high, Capitol Reef is subject to extreme temperature changes. Summers are hot, with high temperatures averaging in the 90s. Spring and fall have warm days and cool nights. Daytime winter temperatures can drop to 42 degrees F, to an average of 21 degrees at night. Annual rainfall averages less than seven inches.

Two national forests west of Capitol Reef—Fishlake and Dixie—offer additional camping and hiking facilities.

Larry Ulrich

CHIMNEY ROCK *in Capitol Reef National Park is accessible by a trail leading from a pull-out on Utah Hwy. 24 in the northern portion of the park. It is a fine example of the effect of erosion.*

It takes a bit of extra planning and effort to get the best out of a Capitol Reef visit. But for the visitor seeking wilderness, who appreciates the desert's quiet beauty, and who also appreciates earth building on a spectacular scale, the effort is well worth it.

Capitol Reef National Park Torrey, UT 84775, (801) 425-3791

Access: From the west via Torrey or from the east via Caineville and Hanksville, Utah, on Utah State Hwy. 24.

Season: Park open all year. Weather occasionally prohibits access to dirt and gravel roads.

Visitor Center: Located 11 miles east of Torrey on Utah Hwy. 24.

Lodging: In park: none. Nearby: in communities west of the park and in Hanksville to the east.

Camping: Three campgrounds open all year, no reservations accepted. Fee at main campground, 1 mile from Visitor Center. No fee at Cedar Mesa or Cathedral Valley campgrounds, in southern and northern districts of park, respectively. Two small group sites adjacent to main campground; reservation required.

Services: In park: none. Food and fuel available in nearby communities.

Activities: Driving, hiking, backpacking with permit, exhibits, interpretive programs. Also fruit picking from orchards in season (apples in October) and an excellent bookstore.

For further information on permits, fees, reservations and park regulations, phone or write park headquarters.

91

J F M A M J J A S O N D
Capitol Reef annual visitors, 385,000

92

BRYCE CANYON *National Park is typified by rock formations like the one above, all the result of erosion by rain and frost over a long time. These formations are known locally as hoodoos.*

Bill Neill

Bryce Canyon National Park

Bryce Canyon is not a canyon in the true sense of the word but a series of spectacular amphitheaters carved into the edge of the high Paunsaugunt Plateau of southwestern Utah. The view from the plateau—one of the highest elevated tablelands in America—is equally spectacular. Two thousand feet below lies the expansive Colorado Plateau, 130,000 square miles of high desert covering parts of four states, one of the West's dominant landforms of which Bryce Canyon is a part. On a clear day you can make out, from a vantage point on 9,105-foot-high Rainbow Point, the Henry Mountains, 90 miles to the northeast. Eighty miles to the southeast is Navajo Mountain near the Arizona border.

But it is not primarily the view that has made tiny (56-square-mile) Bryce Canyon National Park the second most-visited of Utah's five national parks. It is the fascinating geological story the park tells and which it lays so grandly before the visitor's eyes. Preserved here is a landscape millions of years old whose highly colored, bizarre rock pinnacles, arches, walls and spires ("hoodoos" in the Bryce Canyon lexicon) are among the best examples of the effect of erosion on the American continent.

Bryce Canyon has been called a "visual feast," which indeed it is. Its range of colors is astounding, constantly shifting throughout the day and throughout the season: reds, golds, blues, lavenders, oranges, with some colors changing dramatically even as a cloud passes overhead. To some visitors, the hoodoos become a guessing game. Does that strange rock formation over there look more like a Chinese pagoda, a Turkish minaret or the cannon tower of a Spanish castle? What could the first human visitor have thought of these strange, water-sculpted rocks, denied the explanation of scientists? How could so many colors be crammed into such a relatively small space on earth?

The Paiute Indians, doubtless just as baffled, didn't even try to explain them. They called Bryce Canyon's formations, simply, "red rocks standing like men in a bowl-shaped canyon." Later visitors drew names from their imagination: The Turtle, Alley Oop, The Organ Grinder's Monkey. Yet from what we know about the Paiutes, they attached a spiritual significance to the rocks they saw along the 20-mile-long Paunsaugunt Plateau. Even the most rational of today's visitors may well do the same. Some of the formations have crumbled with age, and the National Park Service no longer gives them names. Still, the names suggest what today's visitor will see—and wonder about.

It was water that carved Bryce Canyon's rocks millions of years ago—snow, ice and rain. Though the wind does blow here, it has little erosional effect, as many believe. Almost all of the Southwest's canyon country is in fact the product of an eternal cycle of uplift and water erosion. The erosion continues even today at the rate of about one foot every 65 years. The so-called Pink Cliffs of Bryce are the uppermost step in what geologists call the Grand Staircase: a series of cliffs and plateaus that stretch southward to the Kaibab Plateau which forms the North Rim of the Grand Canyon.

Even if geology is not your favorite subject, the National Park Service has made it fascinating here. The Bryce Canyon story is told in exhibits, booklets and a narrated slide show at the Bryce Canyon Visitor Center. A "must" first stop for first-time visitors, the center is located 3.8 miles south of Utah Hwy. 12 just past the park entrance.

The park has no other entrance, so Bryce is not a park you can drive through en route to someplace else. But the views from the various overlooks along the 35-mile round trip of paved road in the park are well worth the extra time involved.

Despite its arid nature, Bryce Canyon's high altitude (averaging 8,000 feet above sea level) brings relatively cool temperatures both day and night, even in midsummer.

Wildflowers begin to appear as soon as melting snow uncovers the ground in March or April. But summer is late here, and it may be June or even July before all the wild iris, blue columbine, sego, Indian paintbrush or mariposa lilies (Utah's state flower) begin to brighten forest and meadow.

Frequent afternoon thundershowers in summer often bring spectacular cloud formations which add a dramatic backdrop for Bryce Canyon photography. Crowds drop off in fall, when aspens, maples and oaks add color of their own to those of the hoodoos. And in winter, crisp, clear days, a white frosting of snow on pink rocks, and solitude are reasons alone for a visit.

Annual snowfall at Bryce averages about 94 inches (annual rainfall is less than 15 inches), making it a tempting destination for cross-country skiers, campers and winter backpackers as well as day-trip hikers. Snowmobiling, not permitted in the park, is available in Dixie National Forest right next door.

Snowshoeing is an excellent way to see Bryce Canyon's sights in season when trails like Queen's Garden and Navajo, just below the plateau rim, are covered with snow. If you don't have your own, you can borrow snowshoes (free) at the visitor center when available.

Except for Christmas Day, the visitor center is open year-round, and the park itself is never closed. If traveling by car, the park's famous "badlands" pinnacles, spires and monuments can best be seen from Fairyland, Sunrise, Sunset, Inspiration and Bryce Points, all just off the main park road in the Bryce Amphitheater area, and at Yovimpa, Rainbow and Farview Points a little farther on.

Trailheads lead from these viewpoints into the amphitheaters. Those beginning at Sunrise and Sunset Points are fairly short (1.5 to 3 miles), are rated easy to moderately strenuous and lead to such destinations as the Queen's Garden and Tower Bridge. Bryce Point is the starting point for both the Peekaboo and Under-the-Rim Trails, 6.5 and 22.6 miles long, respectively; rated as strenuous, their sights are well worth the extra effort. Anywhere in Bryce Canyon, hikers should carry water. It should also be remembered that all trails lead *downward* from the trailhead; the return trip is uphill.

Attracted by the park's famous geological formations, many visitors are surprised to find that Bryce Canyon supports such a fine forest community as well as a diverse wildlife population. As you climb to Yovimpa and Rainbow Points, the forests change from dwarf plants such as juniper and pinyon pine, familiar in Utah's canyon country, to ponderosa pines on the plateau surface to spruce, fir and aspen higher up.

Bryce Canyon National Park Bryce Canyon, UT 84717, (801) 834-5322

Fred Hirschmann

THE SOLITARY SPIRE *of Thor's Hammer radiates in the warm glow of morning sunlight at Bryce Canyon National Park.*

Access: From Panguitch, south on U.S. 89 to Bryce Junction (7 miles), turn east on Utah 12 to the park's west entrance (17 miles). From Boulder/Grover, go west via Hwy. 12 to Capitol Reef, and the park's east entrance (120 miles).

Season: Park is open year-round.

Visitor Center: Open seven days a week, year-round, from 8:30 A.M. to 4:30 P.M.; until 8 P.M. in summer. Closed Dec. 25.

Lodging: In park: Bryce Lodge open mid-May to Sept. 30. For reservations, apply to T.W. Recreational Services, Inc., 451 Main, P.O. Box 400, Cedar City, Utah 84720. Telephone (801) 586-7686. Nearby: Bryce Canyon Pines Motel, Pink Cliffs Village, and Ruby's Inn, near park entrance, year-round.

Camping: North campground (at headquarters) open all year. Sunset (1 mile south of headquarters) open mid-May to Sept. 30. Park has 218 campsites. No reservations taken.

Services: In park: meals served at Bryce Lodge from May to September. Nearby: Meals, food and supplies at stores and lodges near park entrance.

Activities: Driving, hiking, horseback riding, bird- and wildlife watching, guided walks, campfire programs. Cross-country skiing, snowshoeing and backpacking by free permit.

For further information on permits, fees and park regulations, write or call park headquarters.

J F M A M J J A S O N D
Bryce Canyon annual visitors, 580,000

Zion National Park

Zion National Park has many features one might expect to find in Utah's colorful Canyon Country: water-eroded rock formations in vivid colors, the world's largest rock arch, a deep canyon whose sheer rock walls terrified early Indians, and tablelike plateaus. But it also holds a few surprises. Known to only a few because it is one of Zion's least-promoted features is a petrified forest, reached only by trail. There is a desert swamp. There are tumbling waterfalls and bubbling springs, particularly active during the late spring snowmelt runoff.

To the 19th Century Mormon pioneers fleeing religious, economic and political persecution in Illinois, the word "Zion" suggested a place of peace and refuge. At the end of their famous 1,500-mile trek from Illinois in 1846–47, the Mormons established their Zion in Utah's Great Salt Lake Valley; later, they founded small towns throughout Utah and neighboring states where their imprint is inescapable even today.

In an even wider sense, Zion National Park is itself a place of peace and refuge, a trek backward into both human and natural history.

Much of Zion's impact is visual; one observer called the park "a singular display of nature's art mingled with nonsense." At times, the park seems to overwhelm the visitor with its vast sense of scale and time; even the smuggest human, for instance, invariably finds himself emotionally and physically dwarfed when he sets foot in the Narrows of Zion Canyon for the first time. Or he becomes just as fascinated by small detail—a minute rock pattern or a solitary wildflower clinging to a rocky cliff crevice exposed to wind, sun and rain.

Established in 1919, Zion National Park is located immediately east of Interstate 15, linking Las Vegas, Nevada, with Salt Lake City, Utah. Within less than a day's drive are two other national parks—Grand Canyon and Bryce Canyon—the Cedar Breaks and Pipe Spring National Monuments, and Glen Canyon and Lake Mead National Recreation Areas.

Although some of Zion's high-elevation roads may close after the snow falls, the park itself is open year-round and almost all of its roads and hiking trails below about 6,000 feet in elevation can be used any month of the year. But seeing Zion isn't limited to the automobile or hiking boots. Bicycling, horseback riding and guided tram tours are other ways to enjoy the scenery here. There are parts of this park, rangers stress, that because of Zion's hot summer weather are best visited off-season. The petrified forest, mentioned earlier, accessible off Utah State Hwy. 9 just outside the park's southern boundary, is just one example.

From May to October, Zion temperatures can exceed 100 degrees F in the daytime; afternoon thundershowers are common in July and August, and they increase the danger of flash floods. But winters are mild, at least in Zion Canyon, with temperatures above 40 degrees common in the daytime. In spring and fall, wildflowers are common; a few varieties, like golden and cliff columbine, scarlet monkey flower and maidenhair fern, grow thickly even on almost vertical cliffs where they are nourished by seeping runoff. Quaking aspens stage a show of their own at higher elevations in the fall.

There are three paved road patterns by which the motorist may enjoy the best

of Zion. Zion Canyon Scenic Drive extends northward from the Zion Canyon Visitor Center just inside the park's South Entrance. It passes through its namesake canyon—the centerpiece of the park and perhaps its most impressive single feature—where colored cliffs soar upward on each side as high as 3,000 feet. The Paiute Indians, early Zion area residents, refused to remain overnight in the canyon, so fearful were they of its claustrophobic geology. The Virgin River, flowing along the floor of the canyon, has been gradually cutting the canyon deeper and deeper for more than 13 million years. It is a river of many moods. When a flash flood occurs, for instance, it can turn violent, hurling boulders and trees in its anger. In quieter times, it flows peacefully, nourishing fine stands of cottonwoods, willows and velvet ashes that line its banks.

Don't forget your camera in Zion Canyon or anywhere else in this park. Zion provides some of the West's finest photographic opportunities for both amateur and professional lensmen. From long experience, park rangers have compiled a list of the best photo times, angles, and other hints and have made them available in printed form at the visitor centers.

The Zion-Mt. Carmel Highway runs from a point just north of the main visitor center eastward to the East Entrance. Works of both man and nature rub elbows along this scenic drive. On the one hand are nature's marvels: Zion Canyon seen from a different angle, on one side of the road, as well as the Great Arch of Zion, a "blind" arch carved high in a vertical cliff wall. On the other side are the whites, pastels, oranges and reds of Zion's slickrock country—rock sculpted

Pat O'Hara

96

ZION NATIONAL PARK *is a place of many moods, depending upon the time of day, the whim of weather and the season of the year. Sometimes, the mood can change in the span of a single hour. On these pages are some examples the visitor may experience. Above, the glory of a maple tree in autumn dress. Below, spring rains and snowmelt turn these waterfalls, near Emerald Pools, into a bubbling torrent. In winter, the visitor might witness such a scene as the Sentinel, center*

Fred Hirschmann

Pat O'Hara

photograph, just after a storm. At top right, new leaves of shrubs and trees form a verdant foreground for sheer canyon walls. Below, it's early April and the snow has not yet melted from Checkerboard Mesa, a mountain of sandstone which stands as Zion's most prominent example of rock eroded in time to fantastic shapes and patterns. The Zion Canyon Visitor Center offers a wide range of services year-round, as does the Kolob Canyons Contact Station. Below 6,000 feet in elevation, most roads remain open all 12 months, making Zion an ideal park of off-season visiting.

97

Fred Hirschmann

Fred Hirschmann

by erosion into hundreds of fantastic shapes and forms. Checkerboard Mesa is the most notable example.

Man's handiwork? That's the road itself, completed in 1930. It was blasted in sections through sheer rock and it rivals Going-to-the-Sun Highway in Montana's Glacier National Park and Trail Ridge Road in Colorado's Rocky Mountain National Park in terms of engineering audacity. Among its impressive features are two narrow tunnels, one of them 1.1 miles long, whose arched viewpoint "windows" provide a fine silhouette frame for photographing the natural scenery outside while slowly driving through, inside the cliff walls.

An additional paved road, leading into the northwest corner of the park, is reached only from Exit 40 on Interstate 15 at the Kolob Canyons Visitor Center. It does not connect with either the Zion Canyon or the Zion-Mt. Carmel roads. Yet it is worth the extra time to visit Kolob Terrace and the Kolob Canyons in the heart of Zion's brilliant red rock country. It is both higher and cooler here than in Zion Canyon, making it ideal for summer visiting. In winter, the red rocks of the canyons are seen in striking contrast to the white of snowpack. Here, too, is Kolob Arch, 14-mile round-trip hike, whose 310-foot-wide span makes it the world's largest natural arch.

Zion National Park is laced with a system of maintained hiking trails, leading to remote corners of the park and to features that cannot be seen close up from the roads. Some are an easy 5- or 10-minute stroll from the road; others may involve a one- or two-day backpacking trip. It all depends upon how much time you have here and the willingness of your feet and body.

Park rangers will furnish a list of the trails, including round-trip distances, average hiking time, and the major features each trail offers.

Zion National Park Springdale, UT 84767, (801) 772-3256
Access: From Cedar City, south on I-15, then east on Utah 17 and 9 to the park's south entrance. U.S. 89 passes east of the park; take Utah 9 west to the park's south entrance.
Season: Park open all year. Some hiking trails above 6,000 feet closed in winter.
Visitor Centers: Kolob Canyons and Zion Canyon entrance.
Lodging: In park: Zion Lodge. Reservations through Utah Parks Division of TWRS, 451 North Main St., Cedar City, Utah 84720. Nearby: Springdale and other nearby communities.
Camping: Lava Point, open June to Oct. 15, pit toilets, no water; South (at south entrance) open all year, and Watchman (south entrance) open April 15–Sept. 15. Both have full facilities.
Services: In park: meals served at Zion Lodge. Nearby: meals, food and supplies at Springdale.
Activities: Driving, hiking, mountain climbing, horseback riding, biking, wading, bird and wildlife watching, interpretive films, exhibits and programs. Backpacking by permit.

For further information on permits, fees, reservations and park regulations, write or call park headquarters.

J F M A M J J A S O N D
Zion annual visitors, 1,670,000

Great Basin National Park

Bristlecone pines, the oldest known trees on earth, cling tenaciously to high, windswept mountain ridges of Great Basin National Park in eastern Nevada, newest of the U.S. national parks and the only one in Nevada.

Established by Congress in 1986, the 77,109-acre Great Basin National Park incorporates the former Lehman Caves National Monument, the former Wheeler Peak Scenic Area and a portion of the Humboldt National Forest.

Now that Great Basin is a national park, visitation is expected to climb beyond the average of about 40,000 people that enjoyed it each year as two separate federal entities . . . but probably not much, so it remains a park that is seldom crowded except on summer weekends. Located five miles west of Baker, Nevada, near the Nevada-Utah boundary, Great Basin comes as a pleasant surprise to those who previously whizzed past on Hwy. 93 connecting Las Vegas and Salt Lake City.

Though it is small compared to such cave giants as Carlsbad Caverns in New Mexico, Lehman Caves has intrigued both laymen and scientists even before President Warren Harding proclaimed them a "living monument" in 1922. Created between 2 and 5 million years ago during the Cambrian Age, the caves are named for Absalom Lehman, who discovered them by accident about 1885. Lehman came west from Ohio during the California Gold Rush of 1849 and failed three times as a miner—in California, Australia and finally in Nevada's silver country—before establishing a modest tour business in the caves.

Lehman Caves is a series of chambers that form one single, large cave. Absa-

CLIMBERS ATOP 13,063-foot-high Wheeler Peak get a bird's-eye view of Great Basin National Park in Nevada, added to the National Park System in 1986. Now that it has been accorded national park status, visitation is expected to increase somewhat, but it is still a park that is seldom crowded except on summer weekends.

Tom Bean

99

lom's tours of the underground marvels sometimes lasted 8 hours. Today's visitors get through much faster—about 90 minutes—but the eerie, quiet beauty of their interior (the Gothic Palace room, for instance) is just as compelling. Cave tours operate every day. Guided tours for the more experienced last about 3½ hours.

If you're a shutterbug, you'll need flash equipment to photograph the caves. And warm clothing: the temperature year around hovers at a steady 50 degrees or so.

But the caves should be only the beginning of your visit. After snow clears from the road in early June, visitors may drive 12 miles, partway up 13,063-foot-high Wheeler Peak, highest mountain in the South Snake Range.

100

The road terminates at Wheeler Park campground, one of four in the national park (offering a total of 92 campsites). Some of the best of the park's 62 miles of hiking trails lead from the parking area, including a three-mile loop trail to Stella and Teresa Lakes. From there, it's another, tougher, four-mile hike to the Wheeler Peak summit. Backpacking is also permitted in Great Basin, and overnighters are not restricted to marked trails as they are in many national parks.

Many examples of the bristlecone pine are seen in the park, usually from about 9,000 to 11,500 feet. They live to 4,000 years or more, thriving in weather and soil conditions that would discourage many less hardy species. You may think some specimens dead when you view them—seemingly lifeless, dull gray stumps. But, inside, there is usually just enough living matter to keep the tree growing into another century or so. (Although the bristlecone pine is believed to

BRISTLECONE PINES *like this one are the world's longest living trees, growing to as old as 4,000 years. Found in Great Basin National Park, they usually grow at an altitude above 9,000 feet.*

be the world's oldest *tree*, some scientists feel that a species of creosote bush, a desert plant, may be the longest living *plant*; in fact, it may be the oldest living *thing* on the planet.)

Park headquarters and a visitor center are located near Lehman Caves. A concessioner-operated cafe serves breakfast and lunch from Easter through October. Otherwise there are no visitor services here. A study was begun after the national park was established to determine if additional visitor services are warranted.

Weather in the park varies throughout the year and with elevation. Temperatures can range from 0 to 30 degrees F in winter, with highs of from 85 to 90 in summer. While the park is named for the Great Basin, a major landform of the West which is largely desert, most of it is actually located at more mountainous elevations.

Late spring is an ideal time to visit Great Basin. Its variety of plants and wildlife range from that of the Sonoran Desert to Arctic alpine tundra. Wildflowers of many species bloom in succession as they follow the season upward from desert floor to mountain slope. Mule deer feed in mountain meadows, and eagles can be spotted in the clear skies above.

Great Basin National Park Baker, NV 89311, (702) 234-7331

Access: By auto: 5 miles west from Baker, Nevada; U.S. 6 and 50 are 10 miles to the north, U.S. 93 is 40 miles to the west.

Season: Park open all year. Most roads closed, probable snow and cold weather in winter.

Visitor Center: At Lehman Caves.

Lodging: In park: none. Nearby: in Baker (5 miles) and Ely (70 miles).

Camping: 92 sites in four campgrounds. First come, first served.

Services: In park: breakfast and lunch served at concessioner-operated restaurant and gift shop at visitor center. Open Easter–October only. Nearby: food, gas and supplies at Baker, Nevada.

Activities: Guided tours of Lehman Caves, hiking (62 miles of trails), backpacking, wildlife watching, photography.

For further information on permits, fees, reservations and park regulations, write or call park headquarters.

Other Selected Sites

COLORADO

Bent's Old Fort National Historic Site 35110 Hwy. 194, La Junta, CO 81050. Telephone (303) 384-2596. Between Animas and La Junta. A major cultural site of the Southern Plains Indians and a key fur-trading center in the West. Exhibits and guided tours.

Black Canyon of the Gunnison National Monument P.O. Box 1648, Montrose, CO 81402. Telephone (303) 240-6522. Near Montrose and Crawford. Ancient rocks create a sheer-walled canyon. Camping and hiking.

Colorado National Monument Fruita, CO 81521. Telephone (303) 858-3617. Four miles west of Grand Junction. Lofty monoliths, steep-walled canyons and weird rock formations tell the story of erosion by time and weather. Camping and hiking.

Curecanti National Recreation Area P.O. Box 1040, Gunnison, CO 81230. Telephone (303) 641-2337. Sixteen miles west of Gunnison on U.S. Hwy. 50. Camping, hiking, boating, fishing, swimming and other water activities on Crystal, Morrow Point and Blue Mesa (Colorado's largest) Lakes; total area of 42,000 acres.

Dinosaur National Monument P.O. Box 210, Dinosaur, CO 81610. Telephone (303) 374-2216. Thirteen miles east of Vernal. Fossil remains of dinosaurs and other ancient animals in a huge quarry. Green and Yampa Rivers have created spectacular canyons. Camping and hiking.

Florissant Fossil Beds National Monument P.O. Box 185, Florissant, CO 80816. Telephone (303)

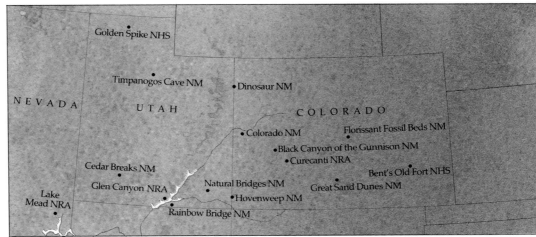

748-3253. Visitor Center is 2½ miles from Florissant. Site contains variety of fossil insects, seeds and leaves from the Oligocene period as well as a display of petrified sequoia stumps. Hiking.

Great Sand Dunes National Monument Mosca, CO 81146. Telephone (303) 378-2312. On Hwy. 150, 37 miles northeast of Alamosa. Tallest dunes in the United States, created by winds blowing through the Sangre de Cristo Mountains over thousands of years. Camping and hiking.

Hovenweep National Monument c/o Mesa Verde National Park, CO 81330. Telephone (303) 529-4465. West of Pleasant View. Pueblos built by pre-Columbian culture, preserved in six separate units. Camping and hiking.

UTAH

Cedar Breaks National Monument P.O. Box 749, Cedar City, UT 84720. Telephone (801) 586-9451. Twenty-seven miles from U.S. Hwy. 89 at Long Valley Junction. Pink 2,000-foot cliffs in a huge natural amphitheater. Camping and hiking.

Glen Canyon National Recreation Area (See Arizona-New Mexico.)

Golden Spike National Historic Site P.O. Box W, Brigham City, UT 84302. Telephone (801) 471-2209. About 30 miles west of Brigham City. Interpretive exhibits commemorating completion of U.S. transcontinental railroad in 1869. Visitor center; trails follow historic roads.

Natural Bridges National Monument c/o Canyonlands National Park, 125 West 2nd South, Moab, Utah 84532. Telephone (801) 259-7164. Visitor Center is 120 miles south of Moab on U.S. 191. Three natural bridges carved from sandstone, one of them 220 feet above the streambed with a span of 268 feet.

Rainbow Bridge National Monument c/o Glen Canyon National Recreation Area, P.O. Box 1507, Page, AZ 86040. Telephone (602) 645-2471. A symmetrical arch rising 290 feet over the floor of Bridge Canyon is the world's greatest known natural bridge. In south-central Utah, reached on foot, on horseback or by boat.

Timpanogos Cave National Monument Rural Route 3, Box 200, American Fork, UT 84003. Telephone (801) 756-5238. Northwest Utah, near Pleasant Grove and American Fork. Noted for bizarre formations created by water in three limestone caves, the first one discovered in 1887. Hiking.

NEVADA

Lake Mead National Recreation Area 601 Nevada Highway, Boulder City, NV 89005. Telephone (702) 293-4041. Four miles east of Boulder. Lake Mead formed by Hoover Dam, and Lake Mohave in Arizona, formed by Davis Dam, on the Colorado River, was nation's first national recreation area. Full range of camping, hiking, swimming, fishing, boating, dam tours and other water-related activities.

101

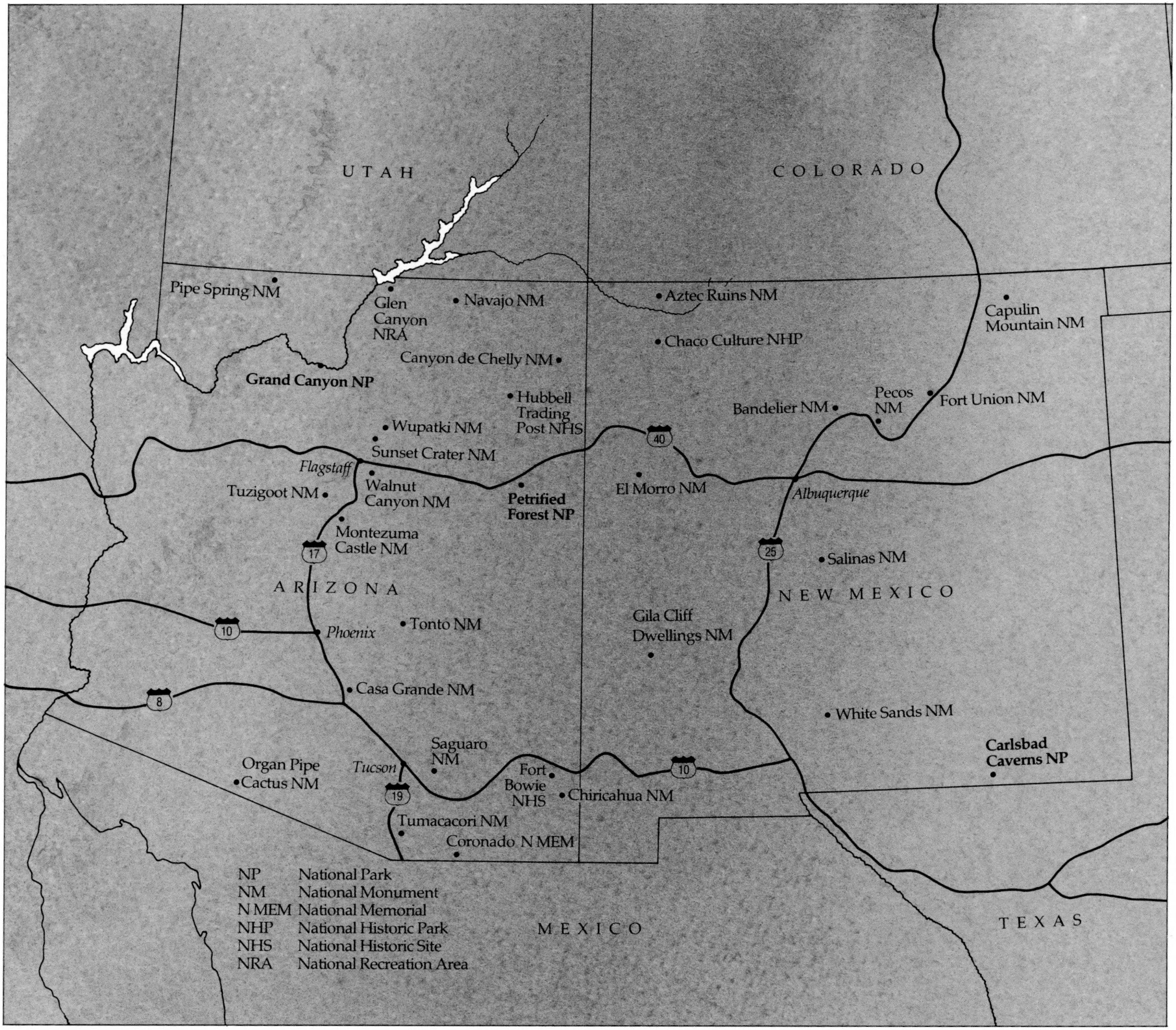

UTAH

COLORADO

Pipe Spring NM

Glen
Canyon
NRA

Navajo NM

Aztec Ruins NM

Capulin
Mountain NM

Chaco Culture NHP

Canyon de Chelly NM

Grand Canyon NP

Hubbell
Trading
Post NHS

Bandelier NM

Pecos
NM

Fort Union NM

Wupatki NM

Sunset Crater NM

Flagstaff

40

Tuzigoot NM

Walnut
Canyon NM

Petrified
Forest NP

El Morro NM

Albuquerque

Montezuma
Castle NM

17

A R I Z O N A

25

Salinas NM

N E W   M E X I C O

10

Tonto NM

Phoenix

Gila Cliff
Dwellings NM

8

Casa Grande NM

White Sands NM

Carlsbad
Caverns NP

Saguaro
NM

Organ Pipe
Cactus NM

Tucson

Fort
Bowie
NHS

10

19

Chiricahua NM

Tumacacori NM

Coronado N MEM

NP   National Park
NM   National Monument
N MEM National Memorial
NHP   National Historic Park
NHS   National Historic Site
NRA   National Recreation Area

M E X I C O

T E X A S

102

ARIZONA & NEW MEXICO

GRAND CANYON, PETRIFIED FOREST & CARLSBAD CAVERNS NATIONAL PARKS

Mountains, deserts, canyons, plateaus, forests, plains—that's the great diversity represented by the American Southwest states of Arizona and New Mexico. These are big states: big physically, big in the scope of their rich human history, big in terms of their natural resources and outdoor heritage.

Combined, they have a land area of almost 236,000 square miles, making them almost as large as their neighbor state of Texas. Surprising to some who dismiss Arizona and New Mexico as so much "worthless desert," their forested areas if put together would be larger than either Alabama or Arkansas. Add the legacy of ancient Indian cultures and it's easy to see why there are more federally protected sites in these states, especially in Arizona, than in any other region of the nation of comparable size.

The arid climate of the Southwest, the great expanses of elbow room providing both privacy and protection from enemies, an abundance of fine natural build-ing sites such as canyon cliffs, all may have accounted for the fact that early peoples built their communities here as long ago as 25,000 years. Why the Anas-azi, the Hohokam and the Mogollon vanished before Columbus is a mystery even today, though drought, soil exhaustion and plague are considered possibilities, and the well-preserved remnants of their civilizations have kept anthropologists and archaeologists busy here since the 19th Century.

As is true in much of the West, Arizona and New Mexico don't have a lot of people for their size. Their combined population is only about 4½ million, less than the city of Los Angeles (although Arizona's nose count especially is climbing fast; its population now is more than double that of its neighbor state to the east). That means there is still plenty of room in which to roam about without running into other humans at every turn.

The sprawling deserts of the South-west, intolerably hot in midsummer, lend themselves to a human sparseness. This may help explain how the world's first atomic bomb could be detonated at Los Alamos, New Mexico, under an almost total wrap of secrecy in 1945 despite its sky-reaching pyrotechnics.

That the Southwest in places is little traveled is as dramatically illustrated by Arizona State Hwy. 666, the so-called Coronado Trail which corkscrews for about 90 miles down from the 8,200-foot-high eastern Arizona mountain community of Alpine in the White Mountains to the copper mining towns of Morenci and Clifton on the desert floor. Hwy. 666, a modern, paved two-lane road, is one of Arizona's most scenic state highways. From top to bottom, it runs for a while through the thick conifer woods of the Gila National Forest, then parallels the scenic San Francisco River, finally unwinding on flatter terrain where the roadside is covered by palo verde, cactus and other desert plants. Yet despite its compelling beauty, Hwy. 666 is by official count, the *least* traveled state highway in the United States. On any given day, you'll encounter another car only about every 17 minutes or so, whether climbing or descending.

Not all Arizona or New Mexico highways can make such a boast, of course. In contrast to Hwy. 666, the Interstate 10 and 40 freeways which carry the bulk of auto traffic east-west are busy highways indeed. On holiday weekends especially in summer, they can in fact be jammed bumper-to-bumper with Arizonans and New Mexicans seeking respite from the desert heat in cool mountain resorts.

There are two other interstate highways with which you'll become very familiar in your exploration of the states of Arizona and New Mexico. I-17 is the main north-south route in Arizona, running from Flagstaff in the north (gateway to the Grand Canyon) to Tucson in the south. In New Mexico, I-25 links Albuquerque in the north-central part of the state, with Las Cruces in the south, 43 miles north of El Paso, Texas. And if you are entering Arizona from the southernmost part of California, you'll probably drive I-8, originating by the Pacific Ocean at San Diego.

Of these modern interstates, I-40 is perhaps the best known and most traveled, not because of its numerical designation, but because it was once the famous, historic Route 66, immortalized in film, song and story. In the troubled Thirties, it was Route 66 that carried a generation of weary refugees from the Dust Bowls of the Midwest to the promised land of California. No longer is the highway used primarily by people who found it, in John Steinbeck's words, "the road of flight." Yet even as a multilaned

freeway it does, as Steinbeck also observed, "wave up and down on the map," thus exposing its travelers to the great topographical diversity that is the American Southwest.

New Mexico is divided into four major geologic provinces, or landforms. The eastern section is a part of the Great Plains, characterized in its northern part by lava-capped mesas and canyons cut by the Canadian and other rivers. Flat plains, canyons and the Pecos Valley mark the southern part.

A huge slice of the 130,000-square-mile Colorado Plateau covers northwestern New Mexico. Here you'll find colorful buttes, deep canyons and lava flows and such other volcanic features as Mt. Taylor.

The southern end of the Rocky Mountains, including a portion of the meandering Continental Divide, extends between plateau and plains. The Rockies enter New Mexico from Colorado and extend to about the state capital at Santa Fe. There are several subranges within the chain, including the Sangre de Cristo Mountains east of the Rio Grande.

Finally, there is the Basin and Range Province in the southwestern and south-central part of the state. Here are found flat desert basins interrupted by isolated mountains, including the Guadalupe, Sacramento, San Andres, Manzano and Sandia Ranges.

While mountains dominate northern and eastern Arizona, desert—lots of it— stretches from southeast to northwest in a portion of the Basin and Range Province known as the Sonoran Desert. Most of the Sonoran, with its unique and abundant inventory of plants and animals, stretches between Yuma on the California border and Tucson.

Make no mistake that either Arizona or New Mexico is "mostly desert," however. In Arizona, Humphreys Peak, the state's highest point, reaches 12,670 feet into the sky over the San Francisco Mountains. In New Mexico, Wheeler Peak, in the Sangre de Cristo range, is even higher—13,161 feet at its summit. Winter snow sports—downhill and cross-country skiing, sledding, snowshoeing—have become very popular in Arizona and New Mexico; the facilities at one resort—Sunrise, near Pinetop in the White Mountains of Arizona—are run as an up-by-the-bootstraps enterprise of Apache and Navajo Indian entrepreneurs whose reservations, among those of many tribes, block out huge sections of these two Southwestern states.

Some of them descendents of the nomadic and community dwellers the Spanish explorers encountered when they arrived in the 16th Century, today's Indians are a major ethnic influence in the Southwest. In Arizona, the earliest Europeans were greeted, not always warmly, by Papago, Pima, Mohave, Apache, Navajo and Hopi tribesmen; in New Mexico, most were of the Pueblo culture. Today, one out of every six American Indians is found in these states, and their presence is indelibly woven into the mosaic of Southwestern life.

Since the end of World War II when thousands of Anglo-Americans began migrating to Arizona and New Mexico, either for job opportunities or for the sun-blessed retirement tranquility these states promised, the lines between Indian, Spanish American and Anglo-American cultures have blurred a bit. But you'll find ample evidence of the historic contribution of all three as you leave the high-speed convenience of the interstate and begin to explore the parks, national monuments, museums and other cultural and historical facilities man has set aside here.

In New Mexico, many Spanish missions and Pueblo ruins have been preserved by the state as well as the federal government. They include such state monuments as Abo and Quarai, near Mountainair; Jemez, north of Albuquerque; and Coronado, near Bernalillo, all administered by the Museum of New Mexico. The state also operates more than 20 state parks ranging from desert oases to high-mountain canyons and lakes.

Carlsbad Caverns National Park in southeastern New Mexico, one of the largest series of underground caves known, is perhaps the best known of federal sites in that state. But there are others administered by the National Park Service not far from a main highway, and they are worth a visit: prehistoric Indian ruins at Chaco Canyon, Bandelier, Gila Cliff Dwellings and Aztec Ruins National Monuments; Spanish and Pueblo ruins at Gran Quivira and Pecos National Monuments. Acoma (the so-called sky city) is one of the most unusual of present-day Pueblo villages. Others include San Juan, Santa Clara and San Idlefonso, best known for their pottery, and Zuni, a center of activity of this contemporary Indian culture. The New Mexico special events calendar is filled with year-round activity centering on Indian arts and crafts and festivals; you can obtain current information by contacting the state tourist information agency listed at the end of this book.

As noted earlier, Arizona alone has more National Park Service sites than any other state. Most were established to preserve ancient or contemporary Indian artifacts (see related article, this section), unique geologic features, or, as in the case of Organ Pipe Cactus and Saguaro National Monuments, unique desert flora which are found nowhere else.

Mile-deep Grand Canyon, considered by many to be the crown jewel of all national parks if for its awesome sense of scale alone, winds more than 150 miles through the northwest corner of Arizona. It is truly one of the world's greatest natural wonders. The canyon and the Colorado River which carved it are now "anchored" at each end of the park by two national recreation areas: Lake Mead on the west, shared with Nevada, and Glen Canyon on the east, shared with Utah. Water sports are the obvious focus of these two NRAs: boating, waterskiing, houseboating, fishing, river rafting are available year around. Boating is particularly big; surprising to many is the fact that until very recently, there were more registered pleasure boats in Arizona than in any other state, including those with seacoasts hundreds of miles long. Arizona has many fine boating lakes, including man-made ones like Apache, Roosevelt and Canyon, all on the Salt River east of Phoenix, first "tamed" by Roosevelt Dam in 1911, even before Arizona statehood.

South of Flagstaff, Oak Creek Canyon is considered one of the most scenic drives in the state. It is rivaled perhaps only by Salt River Canyon between Show Low in the White Mountains and the city of Globe (not counting, of course, the Grand Canyon).

Near Flagstaff, too, are two immense craters formed thousands of years ago; each is worth a rim's-eye look. Rising 1,000 feet above lava fields, pine forests and meadows just north of Flagstaff is Sunset Crater. Its origin probably was a volcanic eruption that occurred long before the first Spaniards arrived. A short drive south of the city is mile-wide Meteor Crater, the work of a gigantic meteor that penetrated the atmosphere and plunged into the earth at least 50,000 years ago.

What is the best time to visit the diverse American Southwest? Any time of year is possible, since one of the greatest pluses for this scenic region of America is a generally benevolent climate. But if you find yourself driving across the sizzling Sonoran Desert in August, you may wish you'd rejiggered your work-school schedule and planned a fall, winter or spring vacation instead.

Most visitors even to the Grand Canyon arrive in summer, since, for some of us, the vacation season begins the day the school year ends, and vice versa. Yet for the off-season planner, the months on each end of summer seem to summon the best from this great national park as well as from the other natural wonders of the Southwest.

A leisurely drive along Arizona's Hwy. 666 in October, for instance, when the golds and yellows of the aspens hint the approach of winter in the high country, is an experience not soon forgotten. Wildflowers in the meadows and forests of the Sangre de Cristo, Guadalupe and Gallinas Mountains seem to vie for attention most just after the winter rains, in the cool of a New Mexico spring. And, viewing its lush pine forests just after they've been dusted by a fresh winter snowfall, who could fault Zane Grey for gushing over Arizona's Mogollon Rim country like a lovesick schoolboy?

105

Grand Canyon National Park

One can only imagine the surprise and amazement of the first human to walk or run across the Kaibab or Coconino Plateaus and suddenly find himself on the rim of the Grand Canyon of the Colorado River in Arizona. Had he moved too quickly across either flat-topped, scrub- and forest-covered tableland before encountering what one later writer has called "the world's greatest Golly Gulch," the abrupt change in topography may even have been fatal. Arizona's most famous natural landmark, after all, plunges about a mile straight down.

That earliest Grand Canyon tourist was no doubt a prehistoric being. Archaeologists have found ancient Indian sites here that date back at least 4,000 years, possibly as far back as 10,000. That means the Grand Canyon was *oohed* and *aahed* at many centuries before Don Garcia Lopes de Cardenas, led by Hopi Indians, "discovered" the great chasm in 1540, only to complain that it was but an enormous obstacle in his search for the fabled Seven Cities of Cibola.

Geology, the science dealing with earth's history, especially that as told by its rocks, is relatively young. Neither our very primitive original American nor the later-arriving, gold-seeking Spaniard, therefore, could hope to appreciate the great significance of what lay before them as they peered down into the Grand Canyon for the first time. Neither realized, for instance, that in the canyon walls, bared by 5 or 6 million years of erosion by the Colorado River, lay evidence of nearly half of the earth's 4.6-billion year history, told in terms of rock strata from canyon rim to canyon floor. Yet it is doubtful that this canyon could have had any less impact than it does on

106

Pat O'Hara

THE VIEW *from Toroweap Point affords one of the grandest views of all of the Grand Canyon of Arizona and the Colorado River. From this vantage point, it is possible to see almost 4.6 billion years of earth history, told in layers of rock laid along the canyon walls.*

those millions who seek it today.

The Grand Canyon ranks as one of the most talked about, most admired, most inspiring great natural wonders of the world. Naturalist John Burroughs called it "the world's most wonderful spectacle, ever changing, alive with a million moods." To historian J. Donald Hughes, it was "mysterious, filled with awe-inspiring power, strangely attractive and repellent, beautiful and charged with meaning."

Joseph Wood Krutch described the canyon as "the most revealing single page of earth's history open on the face of the earth." When he made the comment, Krutch may well have been viewing the canyon from the famous Mather Point, in Grand Canyon Village. If you look down almost a mile from this overlook, what you are seeing are almost two billion years of earth's history. Over eons, layer upon layer of sediment was laid down here by ancient seas, each preserving evidence such as fossils of its respective period. Much later, the Colorado River began gnawing away at the layers, creating the canyon and revealing the story on its rocky walls. In the oldest, lowest layers are clues to the simplest forms of life that once inhabited the earth—bacteria, for example, and algae. Higher up have been found fossils of trilobites, tiny armored creatures that roamed the sea floor half a billion years ago. Still higher are the preserved remains of fish, ferns and the earliest reptiles. It's an intriguing history book, the Grand Canyon.

Grand Canyon is not easy to visit, since it is as much a barrier as it is a scenic wonderland. While in places one could almost throw a rock across the chasm (but please don't try, there may be hikers below) the drive around from Grand Canyon Village on the South Rim to the North Rim is 215 miles—about a five-hour drive. North Rim is the lesser visited of the two rims, drawing only about 10 percent of the annual visitation of 3½ million people. This is due partly to the fact that, being 1,200 feet higher than South Rim on the average, it is closed by snow from about October to May.

But for the visitor who plans his trip well in advance and who can spare some extra time, Grand Canyon is really three separate "worlds"—North Rim, South Rim and the Inner Canyon—with a totally different experience awaiting at each. There are, for instance, several life zones from top to bottom in the Grand Canyon, even different climates; each 1,000 feet of climb is equivalent to moving 300 miles northward in latitude, with no increase in altitude. Such an imposing barrier is the Grand Canyon that many of the species of wildlife found on one rim are totally different from those on the opposite rim.

You *can* cross from rim to rim without driving around. Many trails lead down into the canyon from each side, and two of them are joined by the Kaibab suspension bridge near Phantom Ranch. Built in 1928, the bridge hangs 65 feet above the Colorado River and is wide enough for several humans and mules moving in a single file.

There are places on the South Rim where information is available on the canyon and its points of interest, as well as on current activities. They are the Yavapai Museum, the Tusayan Museum, and the main visitor center, all in Grand Canyon Village.

A wealth of specialized publications on topics ranging from Indian history to canyon wildlife are on sale at the visitor center. The Grand Canyon *Guide* contains up-to-date information on the park. If your interest is geology, plan a leisurely visit to the Yavapai Museum, a short distance from the visitor center, which has special exhibits on how the canyon was formed. The Tusayan Museum has exhibits on the peoples of the canyon.

On North Rim, a drive from Grand Canyon Lodge to Cape Royal and Point Imperial affords sweeping views of the canyon as well as the Painted Desert. The North Rim is a part of the Kaibab Plateau, where you'll drive through superb forests of spruce, fir and quaking aspen, and where rainfall can total as much as 26 inches per year. Winter snowfall also can be heavy.

By contrast, South Rim, on the somewhat lower Coconino Plateau, is both drier and warmer year-round. A mile down, the Inner Canyon is desert by definition; here, annual rainfall totals only about 10 inches and snow seldom falls. Cactus, agave and blackbrush are common plants on the canyon floor, while along streambanks you'll see willows and cottonwoods, among other trees.

Throughout the Grand Canyon area, more than 1,000 species of plants have been identified. Checklists of mammals and birds are available.

Extending both along the rims and into the canyon, many trails give the hiker a chance to see differing aspects of the park. At the bottom, river trips are popular year-round. About two dozen commercial operators offer white water excursions either in motorized boats or oar-powered dories and rafts.

Another exciting way to visit the Inner Canyon is by mule. From the South Rim,

107

Pat O'Hara

108   SUBTLE CHANGES *of light or time of day can*
provide a totally new insight into the Grand
Canyon, whether exploring the Inner Canyon or
standing on North or South Rim. These
photographs are examples of what the visitor may
experience. Clockwise from above: Elves Chasm in
the Inner Canyon; North Rim (both pages);
Havasu Falls; a raft party pausing during a trip
down the Colorado River; sunset at Yavapai Point.
Elves Chasm is one of the more popular side

Tom Bean

Pat O'Hara

canyons leading off the main canyon. Here, a series of waterfalls climbs up the canyon in a system of small stair step pools. The plant growth on both sides consists of moss and clusters of maidenhair fern. Floating or rafting the Colorado is an experience back through time. Many styles of traveling the river are offered by Grand Canyon National Park concessioners. Some rafts are oar-powered, others have motors. Most trips begin at Lees Ferry, Arizona, and can vary in length up to three weeks. The activity is popular any time of year and the rafts are busy, so reservations are recommended.

109

Bill Neill

Pat O'Hara

one-day trips are available to Plateau Point, and overnight trips extend to Phantom Ranch, weather permitting. From the North Rim, mule trips go as far as Roaring Springs, a one-day trip. Horseback rides are also possible on both rims.

By whatever means of transport, a visit to the Grand Canyon instills an enormous respect for the power of the Colorado River. In tandem with wind, gravity and the energy of expanding and contracting rock in the walls of the canyon, the Colorado has done what few other rivers on earth have managed to do, in terms of carving both deep and wide through the millennia.

U.S. Army Major John Wesley Powell earned lasting fame after two daring boat voyages down the Colorado, in 1869 and 1871. Much of the early scientific data about the canyon is owed to Powell.

For the visitor with more time, the Grand Canyon becomes just the starting point for a tour of several other sites of the National Park System. Two major national recreation areas have been developed, one at each end of Grand Canyon National Park, as a result of dam building. Hoover Dam, opened in 1936, made possible the Lake Mead National Recreation Area below Grand Canyon. Lake Powell, stretching 186 miles behind Glen Canyon Dam, forms the eastern boundary of the national park and the beginning of the Glen Canyon National Recreation Area.

South of the park are Montezuma Castle, Tuzigoot, Walnut Canyon and Wupatki National Monuments. Bryce Canyon and Zion National Parks lie north of the Grand Canyon, and Pipe Spring National Monument, which honors Mormon pioneers in northern Arizona, also lies to the north.

Grand Canyon is a superb vacation destination any time of year, but especially so in the off-season between Labor Day and Memorial Day. June through August are the busiest months; December through February are the slowest.

In fall, winter and spring, cooler temperatures make visiting the Inner Canyon much more comfortable than in midsummer. Photographers will find better lighting conditions after summer's haze has vanished. Some of the finest of all Grand Canyon photography is that when the brilliant colors of the rocks are powdered with fresh, white snow.

Grand Canyon National Park P.O. Box 129, Grand Canyon, AZ 86023, (602) 638-7888

Access: To South Rim from Williams, 60 miles north on Arizona 64; from Cameron, 57 miles west on Arizona 64. To North Rim from Jacob Lake (intersection with Hwy. 89), 45 miles south on Arizona 67.

Season: South Rim open all year. North Rim open 24 hours a day from mid-May to late October.

Visitor Centers: South Rim, 3.5 miles north of the South Entrance Station in Grand Canyon Village, open all year. North Rim Ranger Station open mid-May to late October.

Lodging: In park: On South Rim, Bright Angel Lodge, El Tovar Hotel, Kachina Lodge, Thunderbird Lodge, Maswick Lodge, Yavapai Lodge; for reservations, call (602) 638-2401 and Grand Canyon Youth Hostel, phone (602) 638-9018. On North Rim: Grand Canyon Lodge, phone (801) 586-7686.

Camping: On South Rim: Desert View (½ mile west of East Entrance) open May–October on first-come, first-served basis. Mather (Grand Canyon Village) open all year. Reservations required; write Ticketron Reservation Office, P.O. Box 2715, San Francisco, CA 94126. Trailer Village (Grand Canyon Village) open all year; for reservations, phone (602) 638-2401. Monument (Toroweap Point), Bright Angel (Phantom Ranch) and Indian Gardens (Bright Angel Trail) are open all year on first-come, first-served basis. North Rim: North Rim (13 miles south of North Entrance), open May–October on first-come, first-served basis. Cottonwood (North Kaibob Trail), open April–October on first-come, first-served basis. Other sites are available nearby, outside the park.

Services: Meals served in park: North Rim, South Rim at Grand Canyon Village, Desert View and Phantom Ranch. Nearby: at Tusayan, Arizona. Food and supplies in park: North Rim, South Rim, Grand Canyon Village and Desert View. Nearby: Tusayan, Arizona.

Activities: Driving, hiking, backpacking, horseback riding, white water rafting, kayaking, canoeing, fishing, hiking, bus tours, mule trips, river tours, interpretive exhibits and environmental studies.

For further information on permits, fees, reservations and park regulations, contact park headquarters.

J F M A M J J A S O N D
Grand Canyon annual visitors, 3,350,000

INDIAN RUINS: A GUIDE TO THE SOUTHWEST OF YESTERDAY. *Ten centuries or more before Columbus discovered the New World, an ancient people lived in the region of the American Southwest now represented by the states of Arizona, New Mexico, Utah and Colorado. Their cultures varied in detail from area to area, adapting to the vagaries of terrain and climate, some under conditions no modern developer would dare consider.*

Some were permanent pre-Columbian cliff dwellers. Others built pueblo villages. Still others moved about from season to season as the Southwest's original migrants. But almost all left clues to their presence: ruins of homes and meeting places, pottery, weapons, utensils. These artifacts represent one of the greatest archaeological treasure troves on earth.

This bonanza of the past has been largely preserved for present and future generations in 28 sites of the National Park System in these four states, as well as in state reserves, and on private lands.

In all, 17 national monuments, eight national parks, two historical or cultural parks, as well as one national recreation area—Glen Canyon in Arizona and Utah—were established principally or partly to preserve ancient or more recent Indian antiquities whose discovery beginning in the 19th Century almost proved their undoing in the hands of treasure-hunting pilferers.

One of the most compelling arguments for establishing national park sites in the West was the West's proliferation of great natural wonders: the deepest canyons, the highest mountains, the wildest rivers, the most spectacular waterfalls. But equally important to those who treasure the human past were relics left by the Anasazi, the Mogollon, the Hohokam and other early cultures, as well as those of later centuries.

Many of the NPS archaeological sites you may visit are briefly described in the sections of this book covering national parks in Arizona, New Mexico, Utah and Colorado, or in the "Other Selected Sites" listings at the end of the book's five geographical sections. Because each NPS site is administered as an independent unit, it is sometimes difficult for the layman to grasp the significance of the interrelated cultures of the Southwest. The well-preserved Anasazi cliff dwellings in Mesa Verde National Park, for instance, are far removed in time from the ruins of Pueblo Indians at Salinas National Monument in New Mexico. Yet each dovetails into the centuries-long mosaic of life as it was lived here long before the Deepfreeze, the microwave oven, and the interstate freeway; the woven together story is worth learning if only to appreciate the present.

Hundreds of books have been published on these ancient cultures of the Southwest. Many are available in the gift shops of the various parks and monuments. If you are looking for one single book as a starter, however, you might consider Those Who Came Before *(by Robert H. and Florence C. Lister, © 1983 by Southwest Parks and Monuments Association). Following a brief general introduction to the ancient peoples, it describes in detail each of the 28 NPS sites, its archaeological history, and what it offers the visitor interested in knowing more about the Southwest of centuries past.*

THE EARLIEST INHABITANTS *of what today is the Wupatki National Monument arrived as long ago as several thousand years. Pueblos such as this one, preserved at the monument, were built by a later people. They have been intensely studied.*

111

Tom Bean

Petrified Forest National Park

Some of the world's best examples of petrified wood, centuries-old Indian ruins and petroglyphs, fossilized animal bones from the days of the dinosaurs, and the Painted Desert are features of the 147-square-mile Petrified Forest National Park in northeastern Arizona.

The park's main entrance is on Interstate 40, one of two major east-west routes across Arizona, and therefore it makes an ideal day-trip visit for transcontinental travelers. The Painted Desert is on the I-40 end of the oblong park. The southern entrance, just off U.S. Hwy. 180, is close to the Rainbow Forest and the Rainbow Forest Museum, two other important features. Visitors with more time may wish to take advantage of the hiking and backpacking opportunities in two wilderness areas, although there is no hotel-motel lodging or campground in the park itself.

Visiting Petrified Forest takes the traveler at least 225 million years back in time to the late Triassic when the region was a vast floodplain crossed by many streams where tall, stately coniferous trees flourished. It was a time, too, of crocodile-like reptiles, of giant, fish-eating amphibians, and of small dinosaurs. The plants that sheltered these creatures, mostly ferns and cycads, exist only as fossils today.

Washed onto the floodplain by rushing streams, the fallen trees were then covered by silt, mud and volcanic ash. The logs were slow to decay since their oxygen supply was cut off and, gradually, silica-bearing groundwaters seeped into the logs, replacing the original wood. The silica crystallized, producing the petrified logs seen today.

The logs are not all where they originally fell. After the Triassic, the land sank and was covered by freshwater sediments during flooding. Later uplifting of the land cracked the logs and moved some of them about. Still later, wind and water wore away the sediment layer covering them, exposing them to view.

You'll see many examples of petrified wood outside the park as well. You can even buy pieces from commercial outlets as souvenirs; they have been collected from private, nonpark lands. However, all those in the park, as well as all other natural, historical or archaeological objects, are protected under federal law and must not be removed under penalty of a minimum $1,000 fine. It might be easier to enforce this law if the petrified pieces were collected and placed in museums. The National Park Service, however, decided to leave them where they lay, trusting their safety to the conscience of visitors who would appreciate them more just as they were formed and left millions of years ago.

A 27-mile scenic drive extends through the park and has frequent pull-outs as well as eight overlooks which give sweeping views of portions of the Painted Desert. The largest part of the park (approximately 50,000 acres), the Painted Desert gathers its vivid colors from many minerals from which its formations were composed.

Other overlooks on the road include Jasper Forest, which provides a good view of the area's general topography as well as many petrified logs strewn over the ground, and the Flattops—massive remains of a once continuous layer of sandstone which caps part of the area.

Most of the archaeological sites are in the center of the park. Typical are the Puerco Indian Ruins, where a culture flourished about 1400 A.D. At Newspaper Rock, a huge sandstone block covered with petroglyphs (rock carvings) can be viewed from the observation point. The Indians used pieces of some petrified logs for arrow points. At the south end of the park is the Rainbow Forest Museum. The Long Logs and Agate House Trails lead into the Rainbow Forest, where iron, manganese, carbon and other minerals lend bright colors to the solidified wood.

Sites throughout the park tell of a human history dating back more than 6,000 years and of animals that became extinct millions of years before this. Archaeological and paleontological studies of these sites continue and new discoveries frequently add to the exhibits and displays at the visitor center and museum.

In 1984, for example, a graduate student from Texas was exploring a box canyon when he found several bones. One of them turned out to be the ankle bone of a dinosaur previously unknown. The long-ago animal was nicknamed "Gertie," and exploration also unearthed evidence of many of Gertie's companions, including an armadillo-like reptile and a crocodile-like phytosaur.

Near the turn of the century, it was the realization of the region's great scientific importance, as well as increased pilfering of artifacts by curious passersby, that prompted federal protection. The area was established as a national monument in 1906 and upgraded to national park status in 1962. Today's visitor will appreciate the protectionism.

Petrified Forest National Park can become warm in midsummer, with temperatures usually in the low 90s, though most visitors arrive then. Peak visitation occurs from June to August. In winter, snow closes things down only occasionally, and that's the season when colors in the Painted Desert are at their most intense. Winter, too, is a good time for avoiding both crowds and heat while tramping along the scenic trails.

Petrified Forest National Park Petrified Forest National Park, AZ 86028, (602) 524-6228

Access: The Rainbow Forest entrance station is 19 miles east of Holbrook on U.S. 180. The Painted Desert Visitor Center is 26 miles east of Holbrook on Interstate 40.

Season: Park open all year with the exception of Christmas Day and occasional closings due to heavy snow.

Visitor Centers: Painted Desert Visitor Center and Rainbow Forest Museum.

Lodging: In park: none. Nearby: In Sun Valley, Arizona, 18 miles west on I-40; Holbrook, 26 miles west on I-40; Chambers, 20 miles east on I-40; Gallup, New Mexico, 70 miles east on I-40.

Camping: Backpack only, limited to wilderness area, required permits available at museum and visitor center.

Services: In park: curio shops near both entrances. Cafeteria at north entrance, snack bar near southern entrance. Food and supplies in Holbrook and Sanders, Arizona, and Gallup, New Mexico.

Activities: Driving, hiking, interpretive walks and talks in summer, films and exhibits. Backpacking by permit only.

For information on permits, fees, reservations and park regulations, write or call park headquarters.

J F M A M J J A S O N D
Petrified Forest annual visitors, 765,000

Pat O'Hara

113

Tom Bean

AN AFTERNOON *sun casts its warm light across the Painted Desert of Petrified Forest National Park (above). Examples of petrified logs like these were first noted in the 1850s. A half century later, preservation was under way.*

Carlsbad Caverns National Park

It's hot here in summer, the season when the lack of rain turns the grassy slopes of the Guadalupe Mountains to powder. Winds can howl in February and March. Winters are normally mild, but from December to February, snow and ice storms can form suddenly, briefly shutting down roads and trails. But deep below this landscape and its weather is a moist, cool, darkened crystal wonderland where the temperature never varies from 56 degrees, and where ice, snow and rain are unknown.

This is Carlsbad Caverns National Park in southeast New Mexico, the world's largest known system of underground limestone caves, created as a national monument in 1923 and redesignated as a national park in 1930.

You can tour the underground chambers. One of them, Carlsbad, is so large that its floor area equals 14 football fields and is high enough that it could accommodate the U.S. Capitol with room to spare. Names of the rock formations in the caverns suggest the wonderment they hold for many visitors: Rock of Ages, Whale's Mouth, Devil's Den, Iceberg, Breast of Venus.

You can also hike deep, winding canyons in this park (50 miles of primitive trails), view a Permian Age reef, see unusual desert plants and, from late May to October, witness an evening flight of bats so thick that early settlers seeing them from a distance thought they were a column of smoke.

There are 73 caves preserved in this 46,755-acre national park, open to visitors year-round except Christmas Day, with the various caves rated as to their

114

Fred Hirschmann

THE KLANSMAN, *an appropriately named limestone formation in New Cave in Carlsbad Caverns National Park. New Cave is still undeveloped, but it can be visited. It is located near the mouth of Slaughter Canyon, 23 miles from the park visitor center.*

degree of hiking and climbing difficulty.

The caves were formed during Permian times—about 250 million years ago—as limestone was deposited near the edge of an inland arm of the sea. A reef formed by secretions of algae and other marine organisms formed the core of the caverns; layers of rock formed in a lagoon behind the reef, and rock fragments broken off the reef's crest by storms were scattered to the south. The reef later was buried under layers of sediment. Cracks appeared in the rocks, creating the conditions for the formation of the caves. Over time, rainwater, converted to a weak carbonic acid by absorption of carbon dioxide in the soil, seeped into the cracks, dissolving the rock to create the huge underground galleries.

Two tours of the caverns are available. The Blue Tour is a complete, three-mile walk-in trip which requires about three hours. In the first 1¾ miles, visitors descend 830 feet and then ascend 80 feet before reaching one of the world's most unusual lunch rooms, where light snacks are served.

The second part of this tour is the same as the shorter Red Tour, essentially a 1¼-mile walk around the Big Room, 14 acres with a 255-foot ceiling. Both tours start at the visitor center and return to the surface by elevator.

During most of the year, the Blue Tour is self-guided. During a part of the winter, however, you must accompany a ranger on a guided tour of the Main Corridor, continuing through the Big Room on your own.

There are some rules and restrictions on the tours as well as comfort and safety tips. Cameras are allowed, for instance, but tripods are not, and proper clothing is helpful. So it's a good idea to write or telephone the park before you come, to know what to bring along.

The bat flight programs are given around sunset. These tiny flying mammals winter in Mexico and migrate to Carlsbad Caverns in late spring. They fly from the caves at night to feed upon insects, returning to their roosts around sunrise. About 5,000 bats per minute may rush up through the cave to begin their nighttime feeding foray. In 1987, the summer colony was estimated at 1¼ million bats, the most in years.

Backcountry hiking is an opportunity overlooked by many in this diverse park. In September and October, there are fewer crowds and normally good weather, ideal times for exploring the "other Carlsbad," the part above ground. The park is situated on a broad escarpment on the northeast slopes of the Guadalupe Mountains. The shape of the escarpment had created wide variations in temperature, soil, sunlight and moisture. This in turn stimulates a wide variety of life forms.

Creosote and other drought-resistant shrubs grow on the flatlands near the base of the mountains; black walnut, hackberry and desert willow are found in the canyons. Canyon walls are covered with agave, yucca, sotol, ocotillo and desert grasses. Juniper, pine and Texas madrone cluster at higher elevations. In all, Carlsbad supports more than 600 plant species in an elevation range from 3,600 to 6,350 feet.

The park has many species of mammals, ranging from gophers and skunks to coyotes, badgers and bobcats. There are more than 200 species of birds, from tiny hummingbirds to golden eagles.

Guadalupe Mountains National Park in Texas is only 42 miles from Carlsbad Caverns. Many facilities for camping, hiking and backpacking are available here, as they are in the Lincoln National Forest, northwest of Carlsbad National Park. If you have time, plan a visit, too, to the Living Desert State Park near the New Mexico town of Carlsbad. It includes a zoo where you may see more than 50 species of desert mammals.

Carlsbad Caverns National Park 3225 National Parks Hwy., Carlsbad, NM 88220, (505) 785-2232

Access: Park is 20 miles southwest of Carlsbad, New Mexico, on U.S. 62-180 and 150 miles east of El Paso, Texas on U.S. 62-180.

Season: Park is open year-round except Christmas Day.

Visitor Center: Located near park entrance 7 miles west of Highway 62-180.

Lodging: In park: none. Nearby: Whites City, 7 miles, and Carlsbad, 27 miles.

Camping: No facilities in the park. Private campgrounds at Whites City and in Carlsbad.

Services: In park: meals served in the visitor center and underground in the caverns. Food and supplies available nearby in Whites City and Carlsbad.

Activities: Photography, cave tours, nature walks, exhibits, bat flight programs nightly in summer, primitive lantern trips into New Cave.

For further information on permits, fees, reservations and park regulations, write or call park headquarters.

115

J F M A M J J A S O N D
Carlsbad Caverns annual visitors, 755,000

Other Selected Sites

ARIZONA

Canyon de Chelly National Monument P.O. Box 588, Chinle, AZ 86503. Telephone (602) 674-5436. Northeast Arizona. Ruins of Indian villages built from 4th to 14th Centuries located at the base of cliffs and in canyon wall caves. Contemporary Navajo Indians reside and farm in the region. Camping and hiking.

Casa Grande National Monument. P.O. Box 518, Coolidge, AZ 85228. Telephone (602) 723-3172. Halfway between Phoenix and Tucson on Arizona Hwy. 87. Ruins of a massive four-story building constructed by Gila Valley farmers 600 years ago.

Chiricahua National Monument Dos Cabezas Route, Box 6500, Willcox, AZ 85643. Telephone (602) 824-3560. Thirty-six miles south of Willcox on Arizona Hwy. 186 and 181. Volcanoes created varied rock formations here millions of years ago. Camping and hiking.

Coronado National Memorial Rural Route 2, Box 126, Hereford, AZ 85615. Telephone (602) 366-5515. Twenty-two miles south of Sierra Vista in southeastern Arizona. Commemorates Hispanic heritage and earliest European exploration of the American Southwest with exhibits, tours, hiking and a Hispanic-Anglo-Indian cultural festival each April.

Fort Bowie National Historic Site P.O. Box 158, Bowie, AZ 85605. Telephone (602) 847-2500. Reached only by foot trail in Apache Pass near Willcox in southeastern Arizona. Site of a fort established in 1862 as base for military operations against the Chiricahua Apache chief Geronimo.

Glen Canyon National Recreation Area P.O. Box 1507, Page, AZ 86040. Telephone (602) 645-2471. Headquarters is in Page, Arizona; Visitor Center at Glen Canyon Dam, two miles from Page on U.S. Hwy. 89. Lake Powell reaches 189 miles behind Glen Canyon Dam. Full range of recreation activities, fishing, camping, hiking and tours.

Hubbell Trading Post National Historic Site P.O. Box 150, Ganado, AZ 86505. Telephone (602) 755-3475 or 755-3477. On Navajo Indian Reservation, one mile west of Ganado, Arizona and 55 miles northwest of Gallup, New Mexico. A still-active, century-old trading post. Illustrates the influence of traders on the Indian way of life.

Montezuma Castle National Monument P.O. Box 219, Camp Verde, AZ 86322. Telephone (602) 567-3322. Visitor Center is 2½ miles off Interstate 17, 5 miles north of Camp Verde. Five-story, 20-room pueblo is one of the best preserved of all Southwest Indian cliff dwellings, built over 700 years ago. Montezuma Well, a separate exhibit, is 10½ miles north of the Castle.

Navajo National Monument HC 71 Box 3, Tonalea, AZ 86044. Telephone (602) 672-2366 or 672-2367. Northeastern Arizona, southeast of Lake Powell and the Glen Canyon Recreation Area. Three of the best-preserved cliff dwellings existing: Betatakin, Keet Seel and Inscription House. Camping and hiking.

Organ Pipe Cactus National Monument Route 1, Box 100, Ajo, AZ 85321. Telephone (602) 387-6849. On the border between the United States and Mexico, south of Phoenix, west of Tucson. Protects plants and animals of the Sonoran Desert unknown anywhere else. Faint traces of a historic trail. Camping and hiking.

Pipe Spring National Monument Moccasin, AZ 86022. Telephone (602) 643-7105. Fourteen miles west of Fredonia, Arizona. Built by Mormon pioneers in the 1860s, a historic fort and other structures.

Saguaro National Monument Rt. 8, Box 695, Tucson, AZ 85730. Telephone (602) 296-8576. Hiking on Old Spanish Trail two miles east of Tucson. Displays giant (to 40 feet) saguaro cacti found only in Sonoran Desert of southern Arizona and northern Mexico.

Sunset Crater National Monument Route 3, Box 149, Flagstaff, AZ 86001. Telephone (602) 527-7042. North of Flagstaff in north-central Arizona. A volcanic cinder cone and summit crater formed about 1100 A.D. Camping.

Tonto National Monument P.O. Box 707, Roosevelt, AZ 85545. Telephone (602) 467-2241. Northeast of Phoenix on the scenic Apache Trail. Preserved cliff dwellings occupied in the 14th Century by the Salado Indians.

Tumacacori National Monument P.O. Box 67, Tumacacori, AZ 85640. Telephone (602) 398-2341. Forty-five miles south of Tucson on I-19. A historic Spanish Catholic mission near the site of a visit by Jesuit Father Kino in 1691.

Tuzigoot National Monument P.O. Box 68, Clarkdale, AZ 86324. Telephone (602) 634-5564. Two miles east of Clarkdale in north-central Arizona. Excavated ruins of a large Indian pueblo which flourished between 1100 and 1450 A.D. in the Verde Valley.

Walnut Canyon National Monument Walnut Canyon Rd., Flagstaff, AZ 86001. Telephone (602) 526-3367. Eight miles east of Flagstaff. Sinagua Indians built these cliff dwellings about 800 years ago in shallow caves under ledges of sandstone. Hiking.

Wupatki National Monument H.C. 33 Box 444A, Flagstaff, AZ 86001. Telephone (602) 527-7040. Visitor Center on a loop road connecting the monument with Sunset Crater. Farming Indians built these pueblo ruins about 1065 A.D. Today's Hopi Indians may be their descendents. Hiking.

NEW MEXICO

Aztec Ruins National Monument P.O. Box 640, Aztec, NM 87410. Telephone (505) 334-6174. Northwest of Aztec in northwestern New Mexico. Ruins of a large Pueblo Indian community of about the 12th Century have been excavated. Despite the name, they are not related to Mexico's Aztec culture.

Bandelier National Monument Los Alamos, NM 87544. Telephone (505) 672-3861. Forty-six miles west of Santa Fe. Several cliff houses built by the Pueblo Indians in the 15th Century. Camping and hiking.

Capulin Mountain National Monument Capulin, NM 88414. Telephone (505) 278-2201. Northeast corner of New Mexico. A symmetrical cinder cone exem-